MARVELOUS MANDALA COLORING BOOK

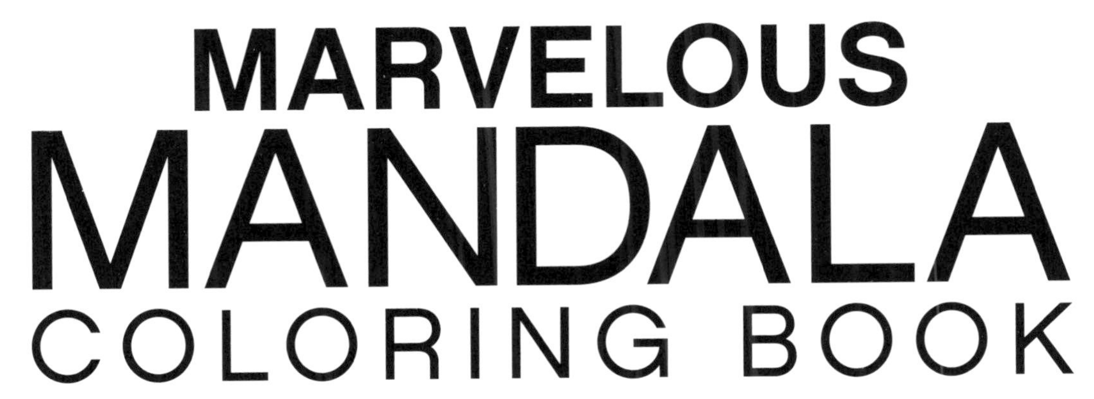
MARVELOUS
MANDALA
COLORING BOOK
Fabulous images to free your mind

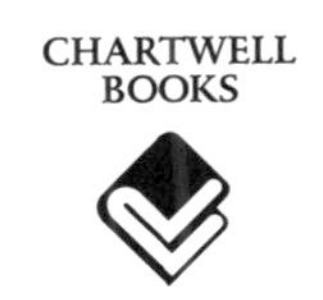
CHARTWELL
BOOKS

This edition published in 2015 by
CHARTWELL BOOKS
an imprint of Book Sales
a division of Quarto Publishing Group USA Inc.
142 West 36th Street, 4th Floor
New York, New York 10018
USA

ISBN: 978-0-7858-3373-4
AD004702NT

Printed in China

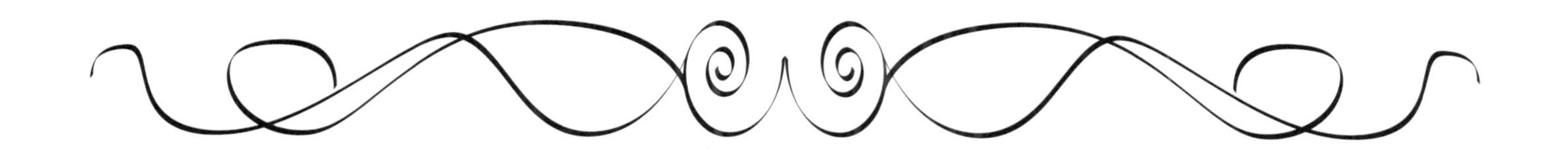

INTRODUCTION

This wonderful coloring book features mandala designs of various styles and levels of complexity for you to personalize and make your own. The word mandala comes from the ancient Sanskrit language and loosely means "circle," "center," or "wheel." It's a simple geometric shape with no beginning or end and it can be seen in all aspects of life—from the design of a snowflake to the sun in the sky.

Although it sounds incredible, you can improve your well-being by coloring mandalas. Within its circular shape the mandala has the power to promote relaxation, balance the body's energies, increase self-awareness, and enhance creativity and self-expression. By focusing on this activity, your mental state becomes calmer, your breathing and heart rate slow down, and tension is reduced.

The benefits to be gained from coloring mandalas are extraordinary, and there are no rules—just let your imagination be your guide.

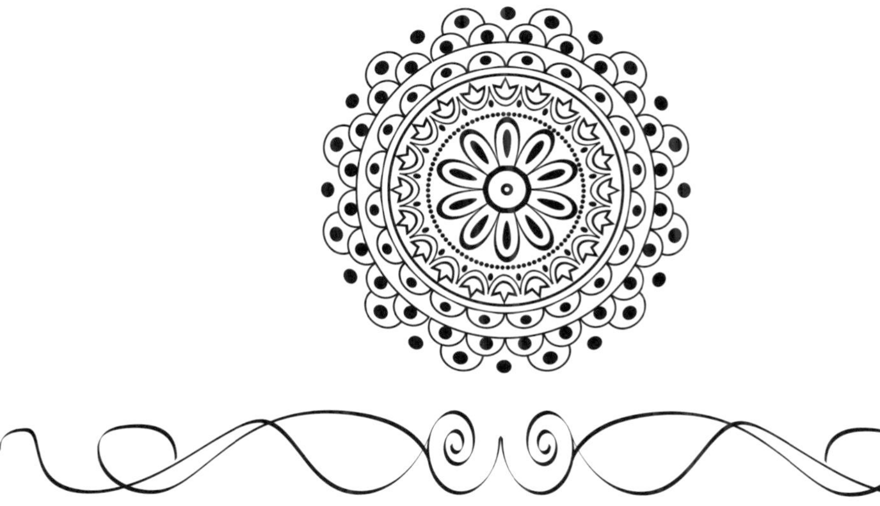

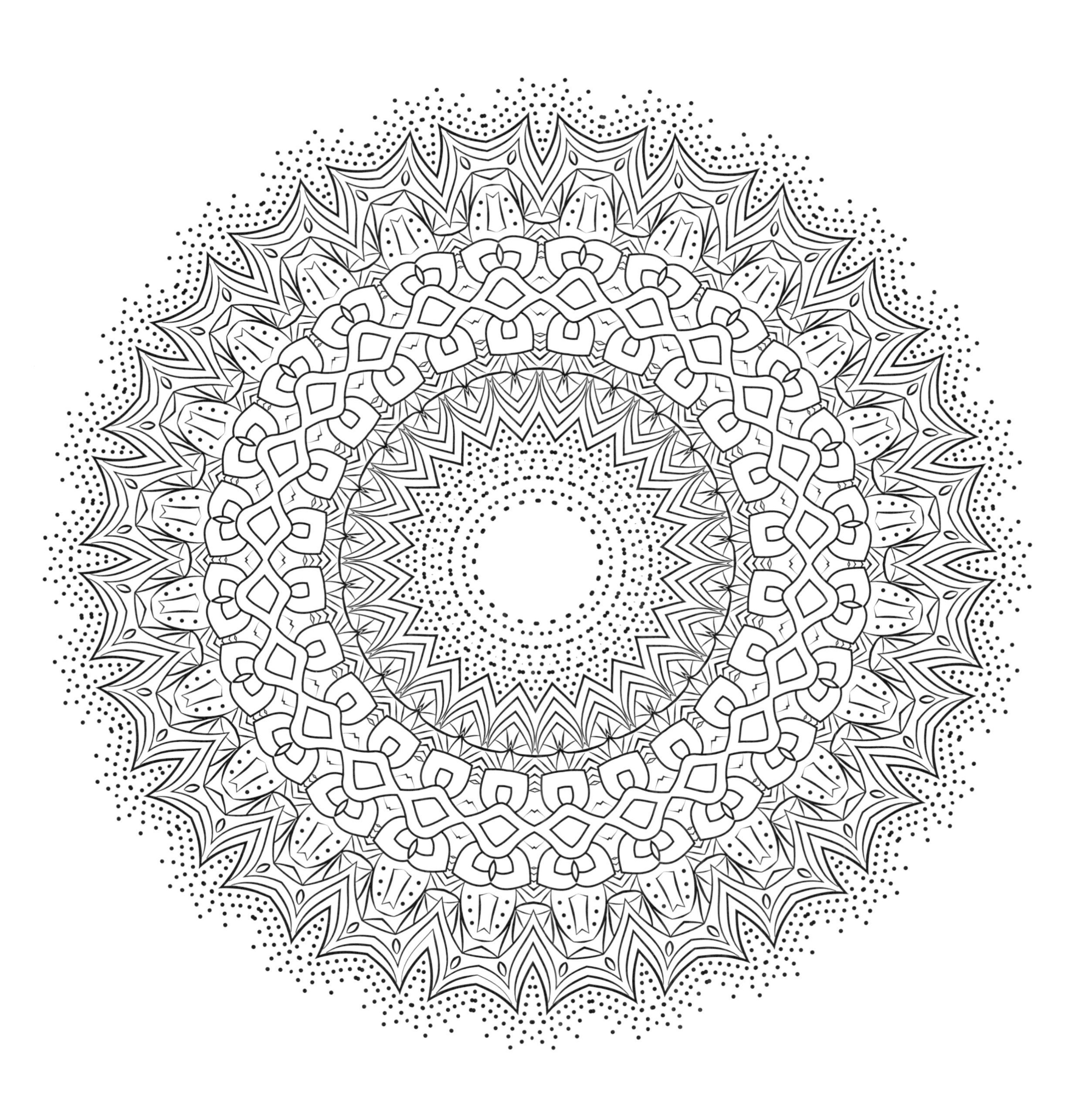

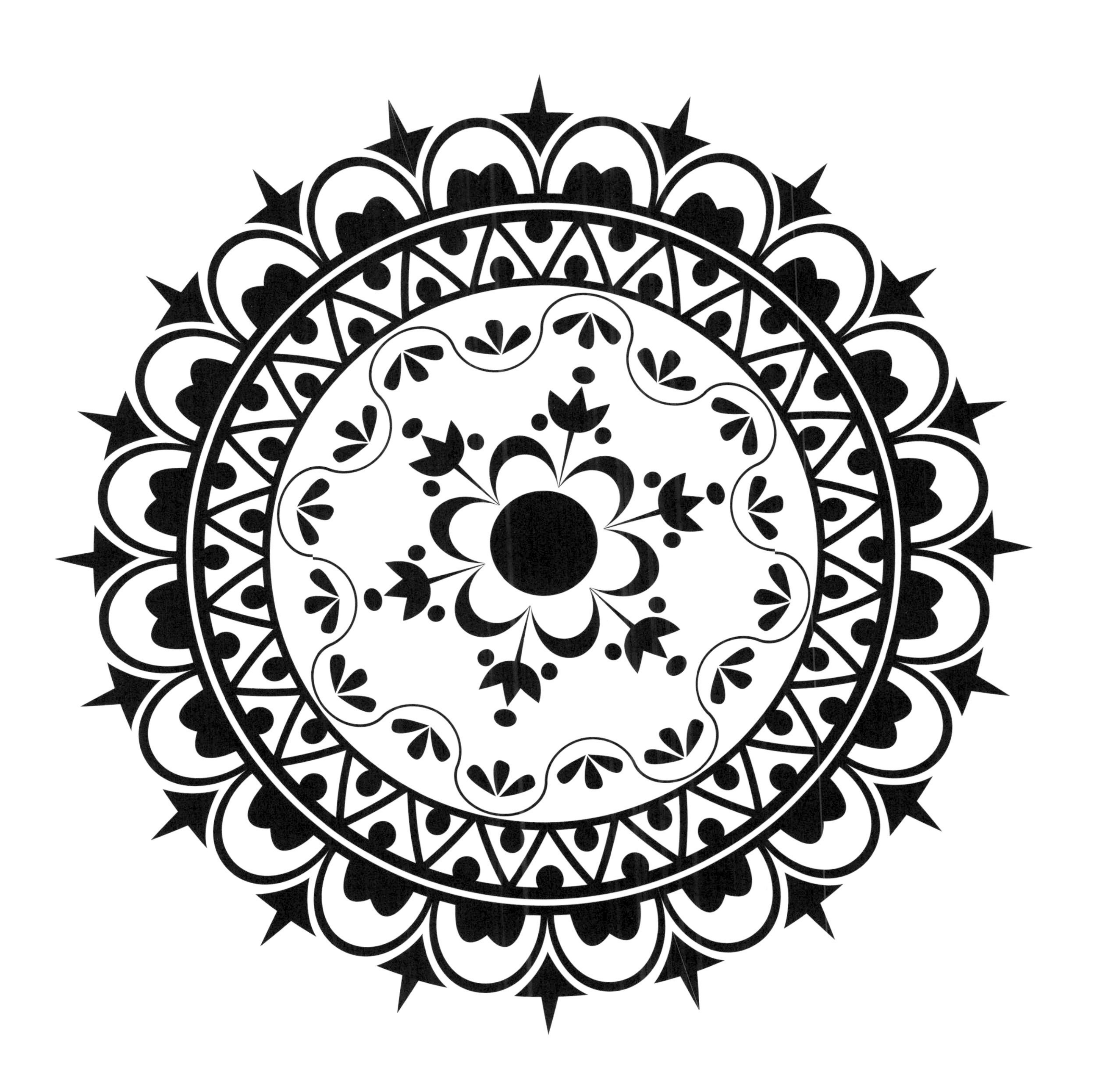

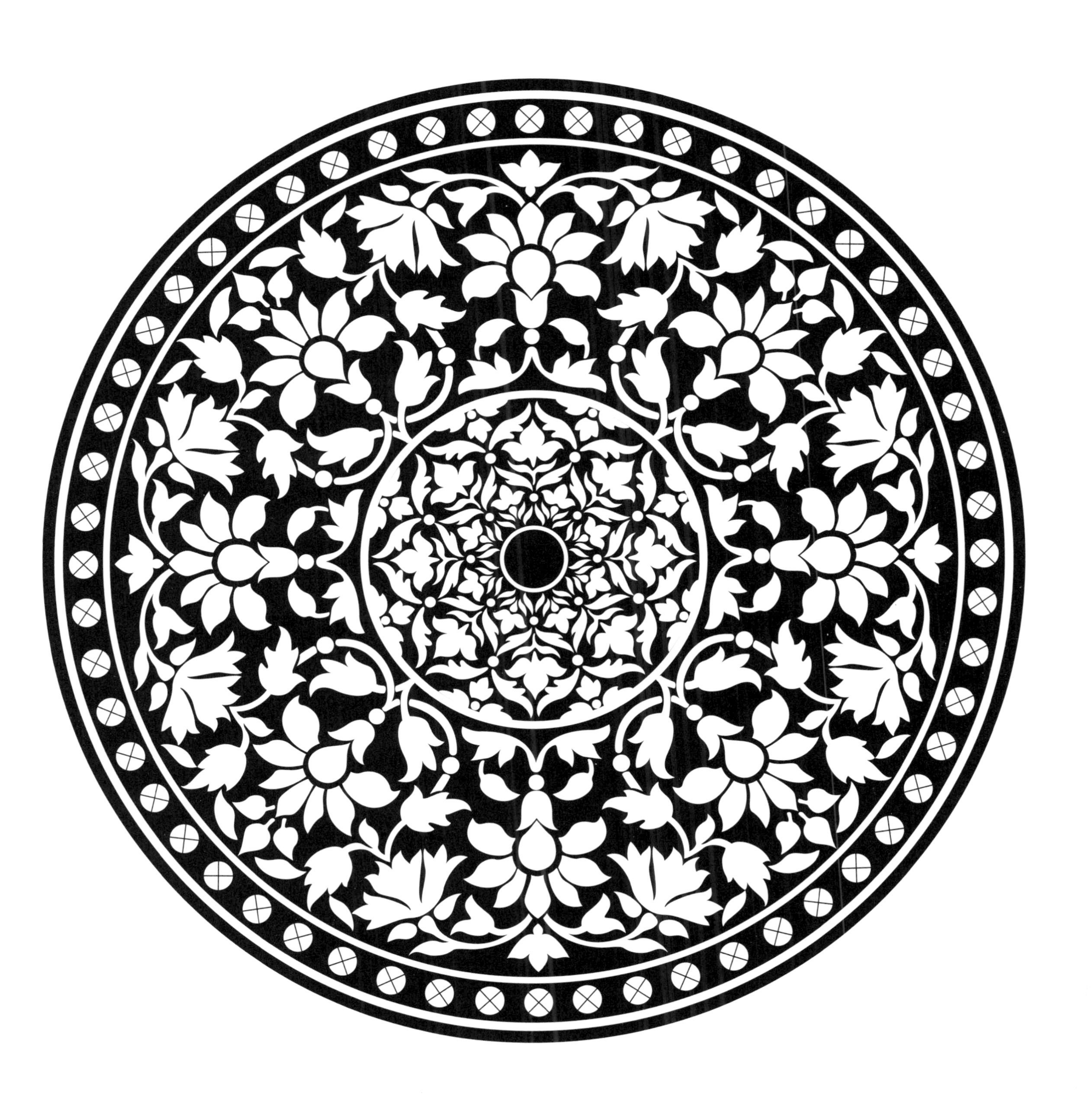

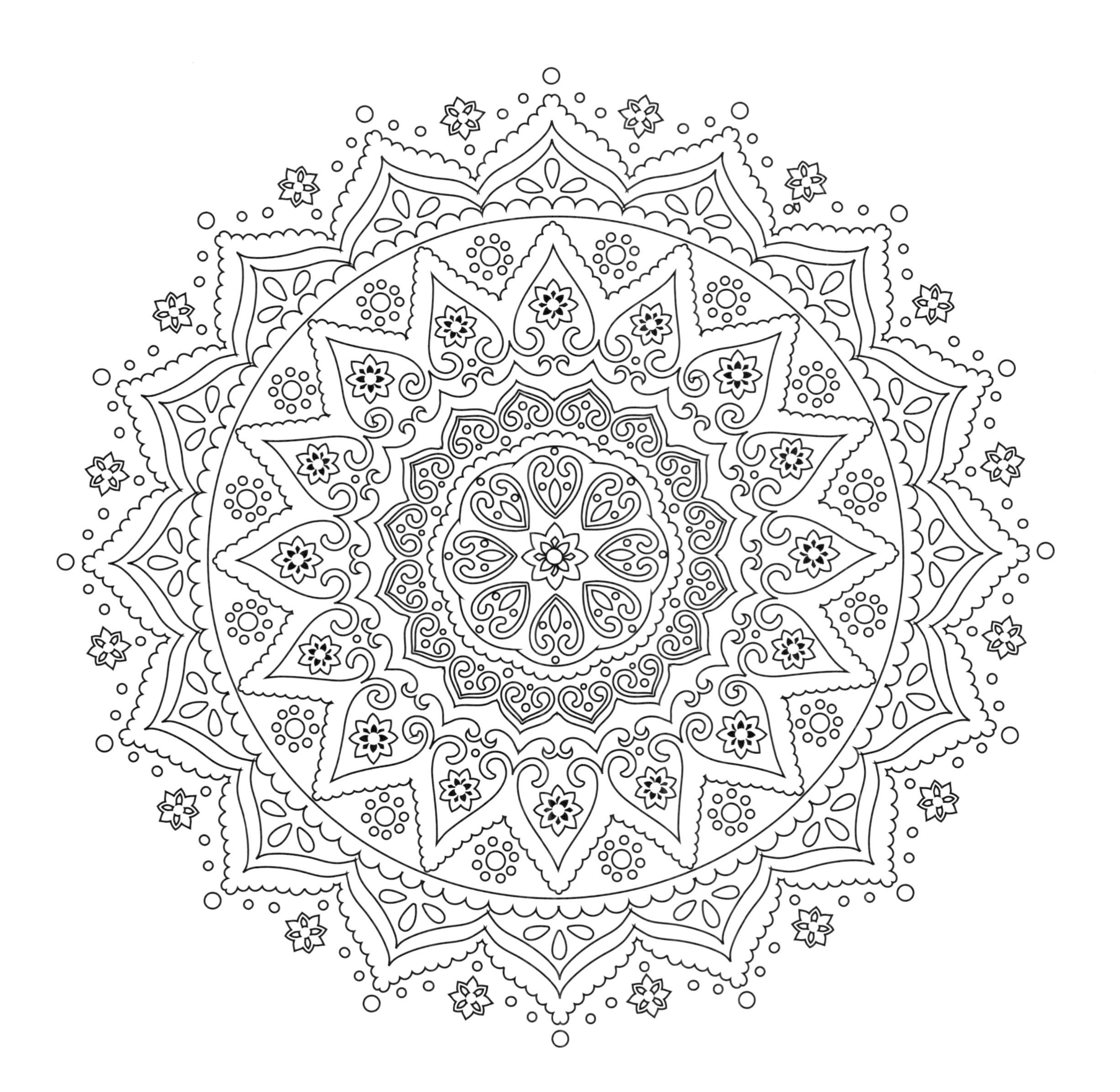

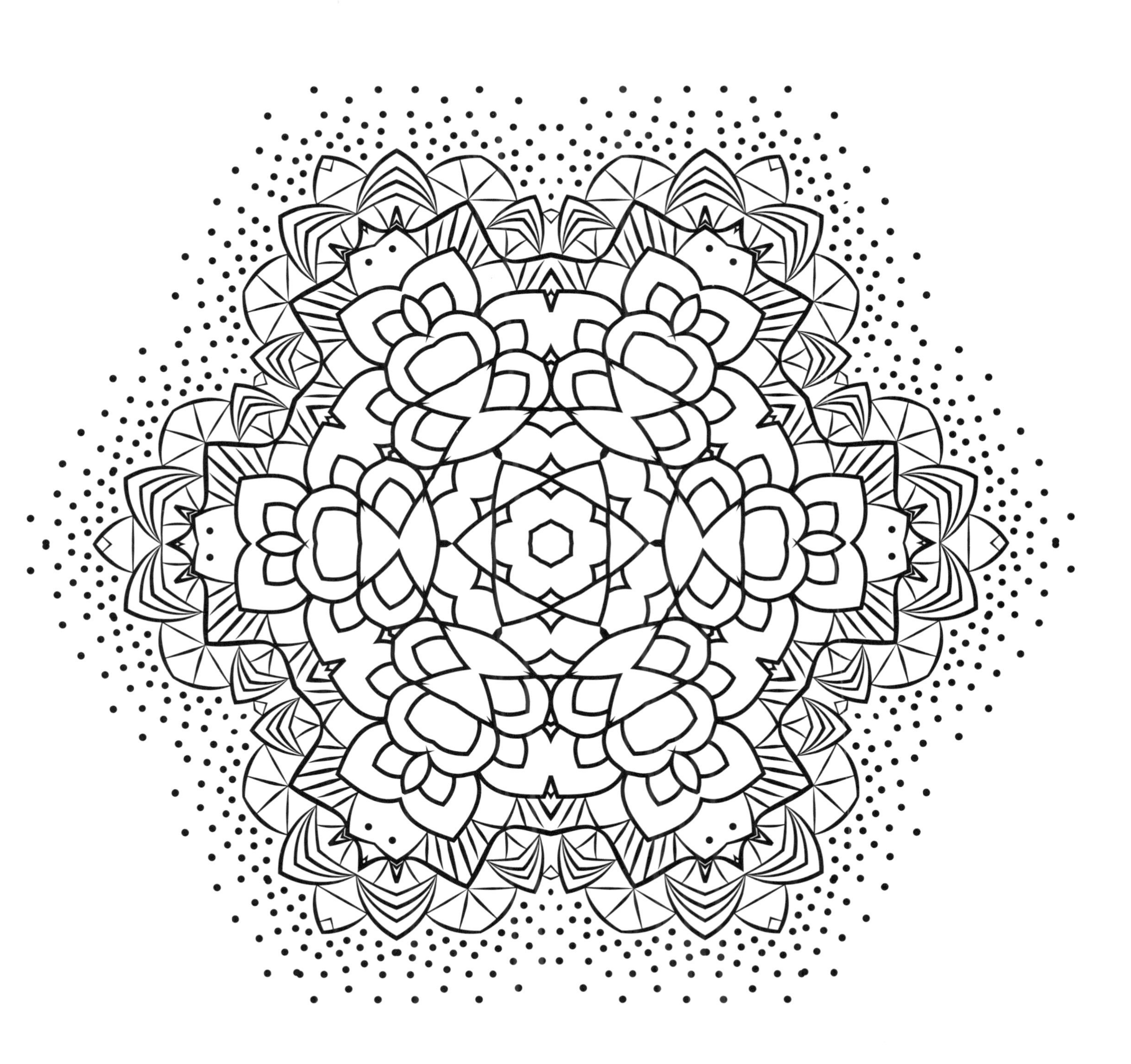

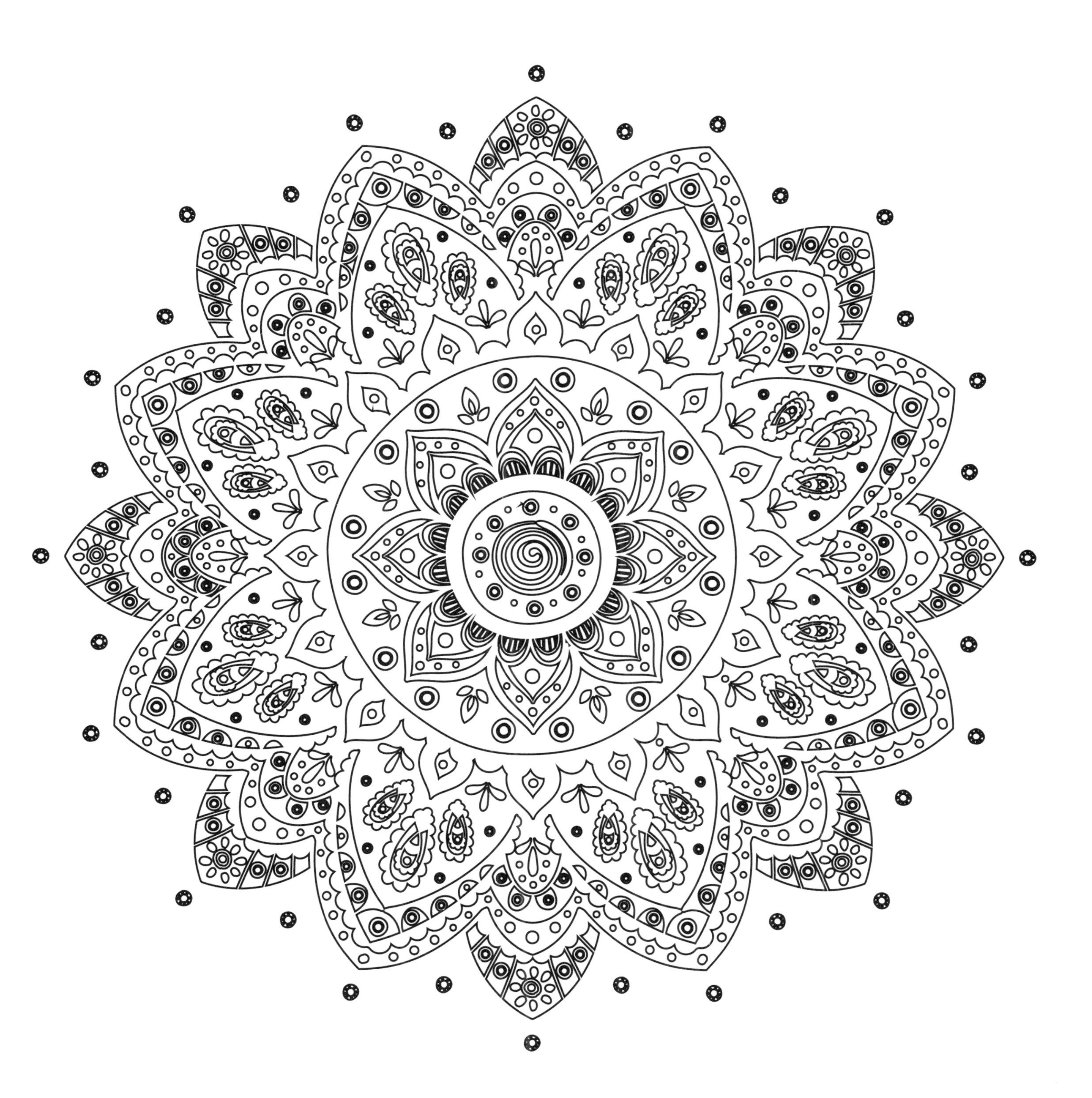

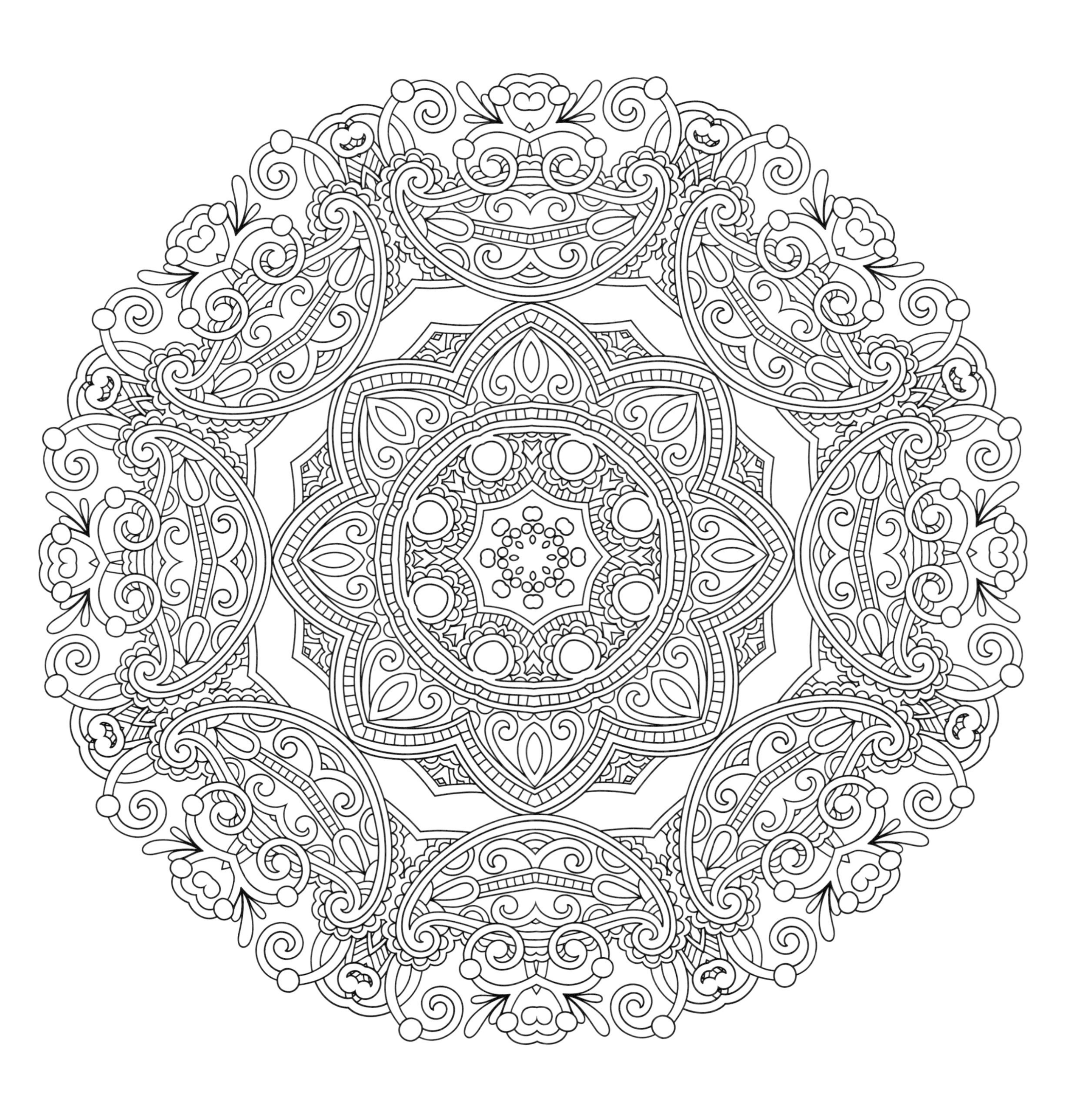

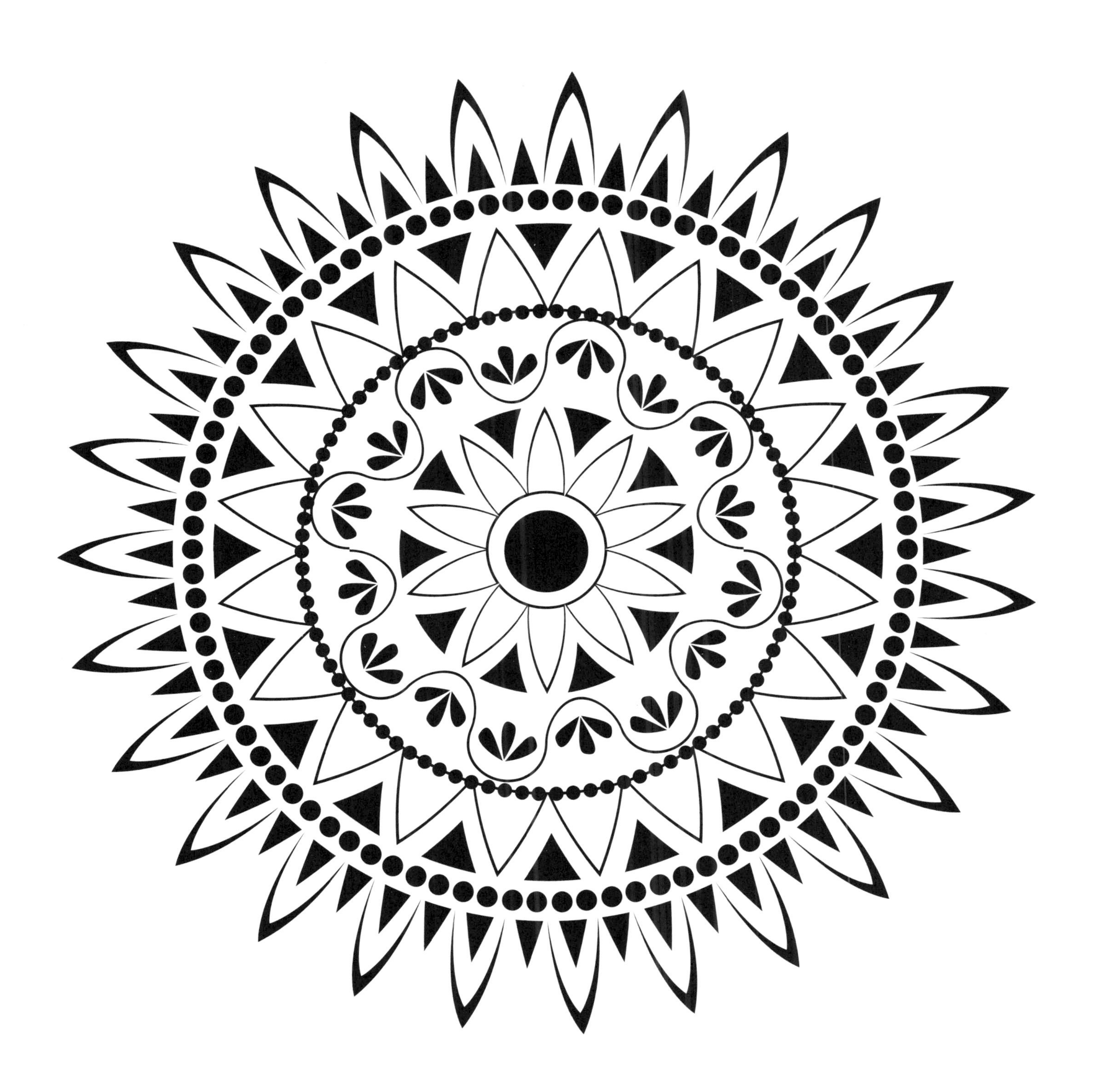

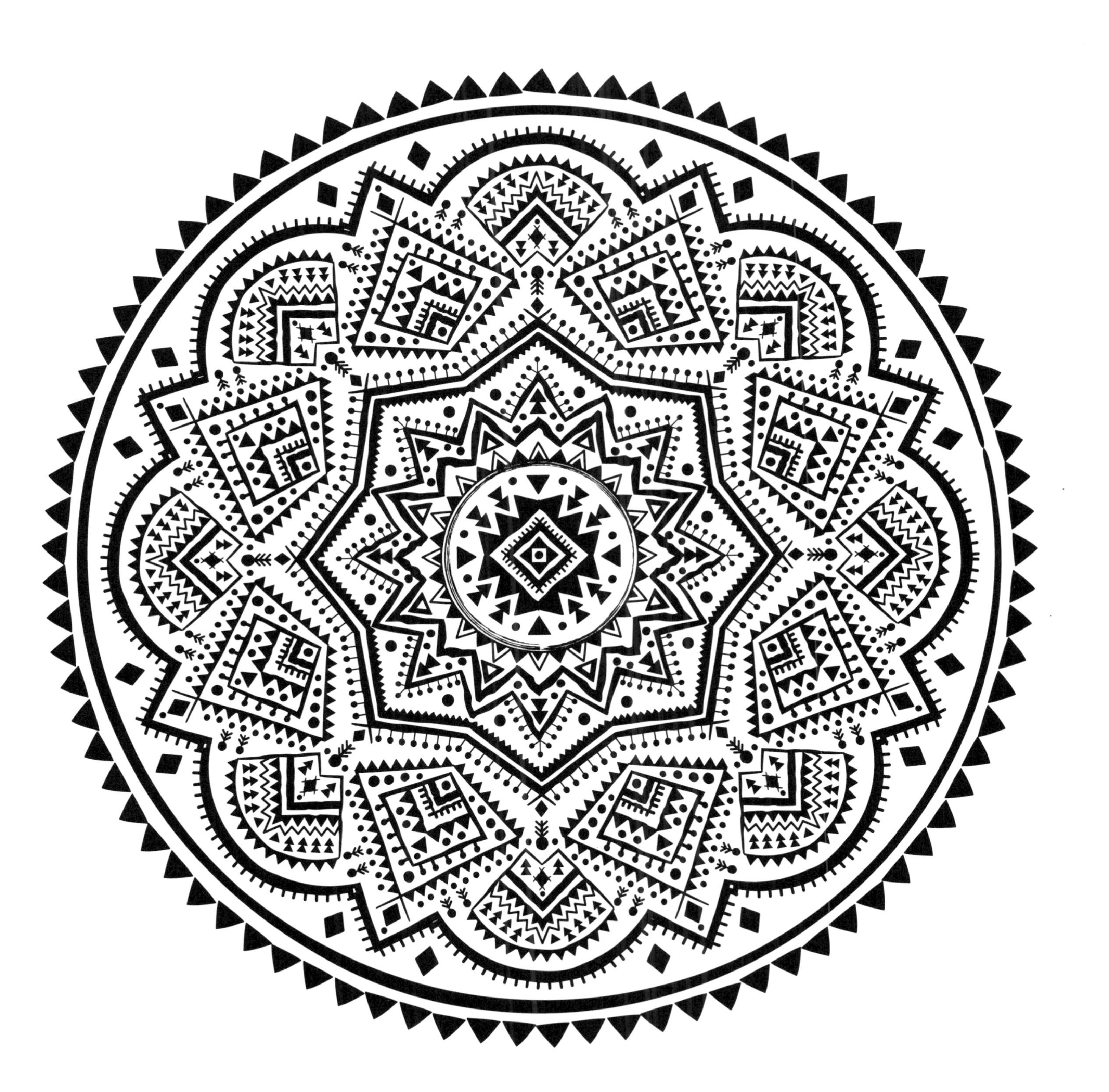

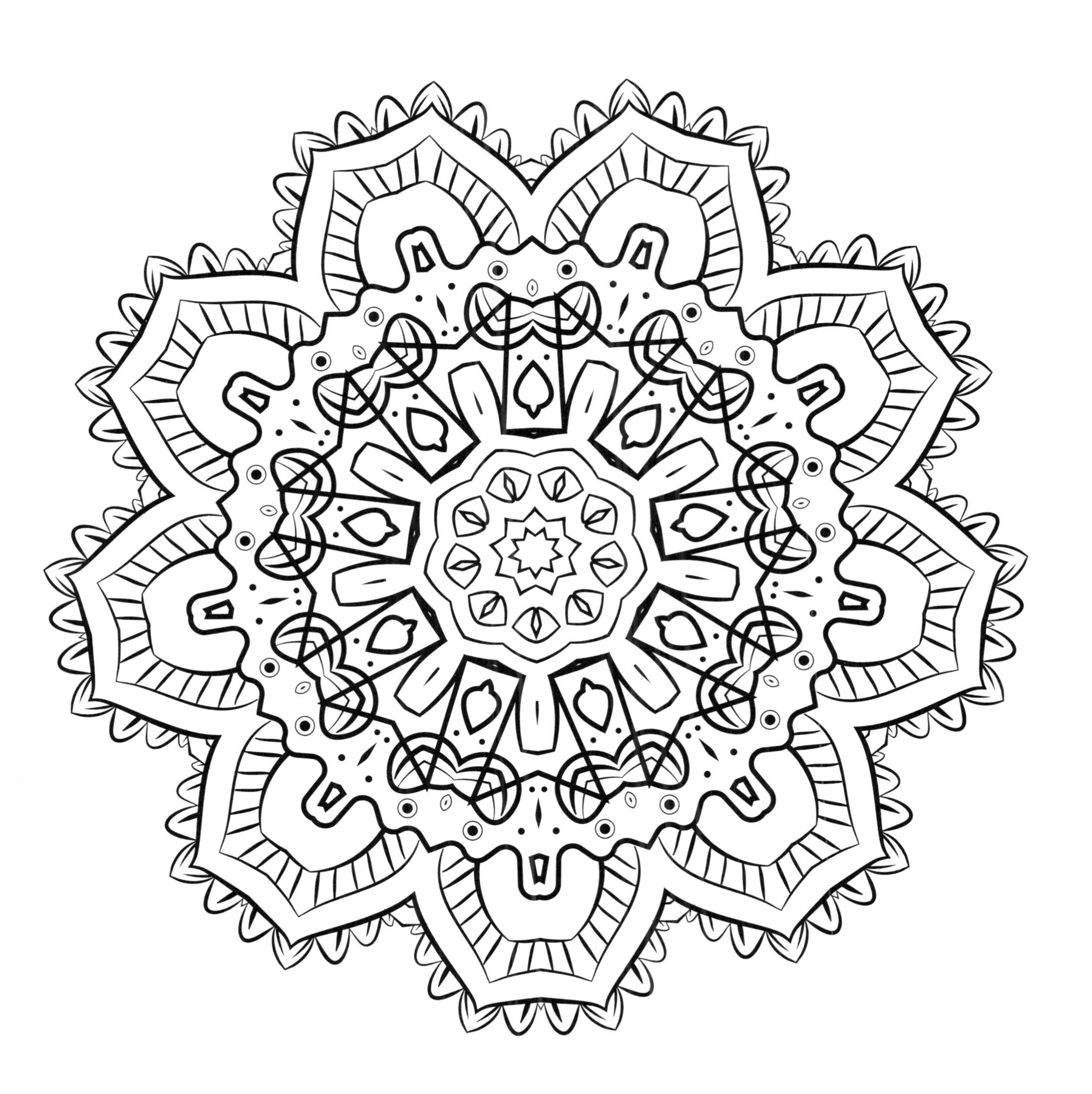

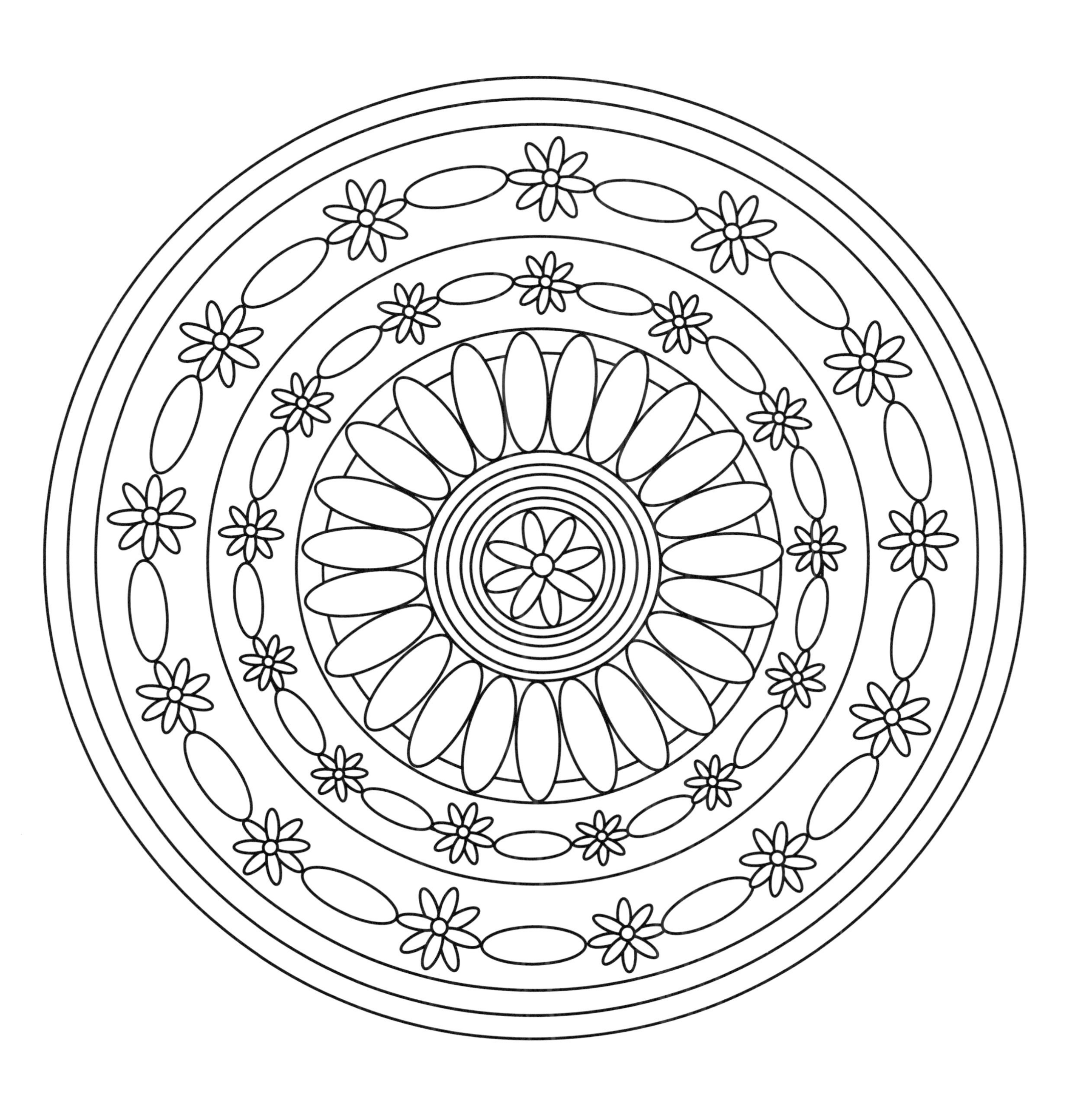

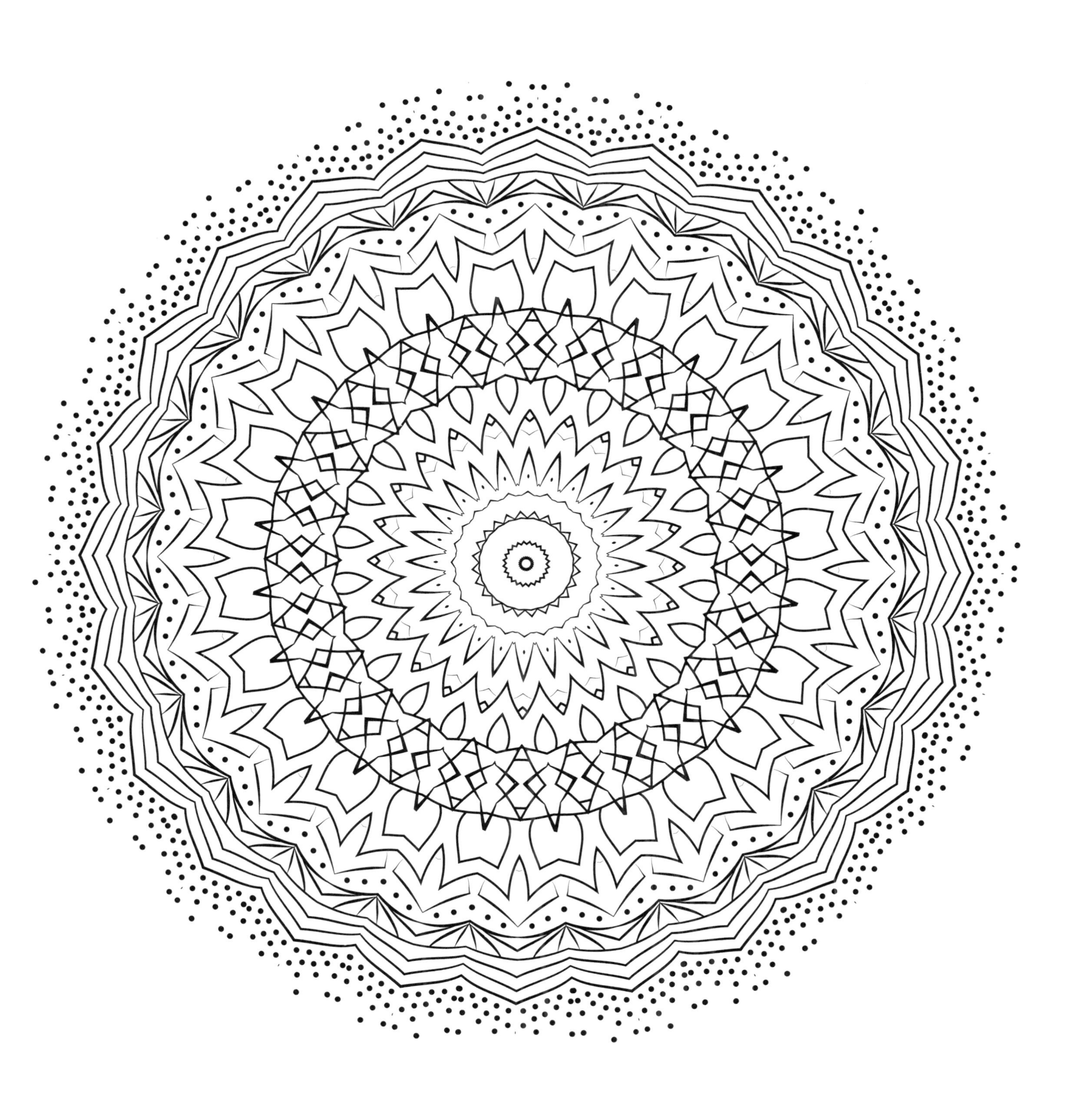

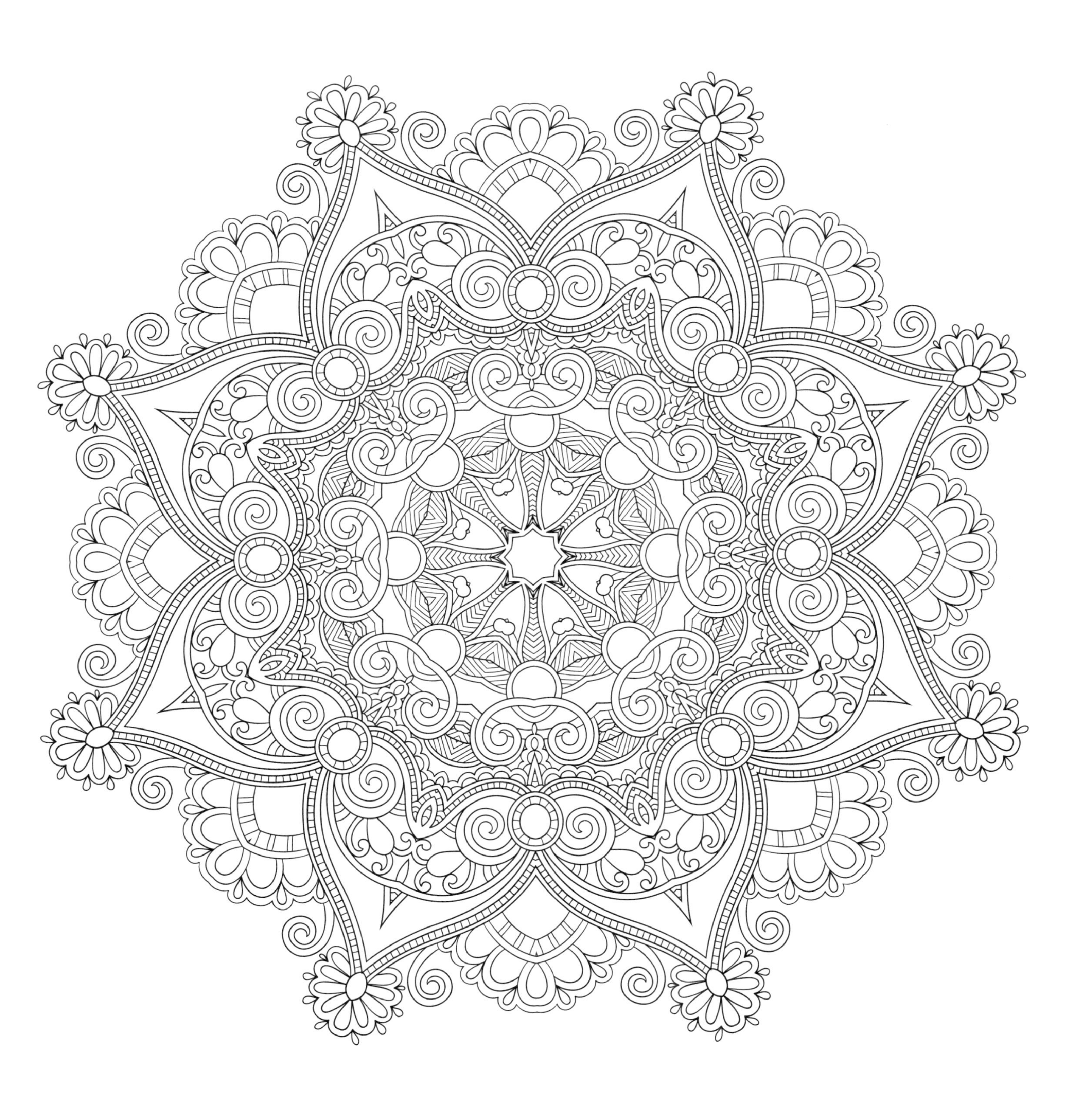

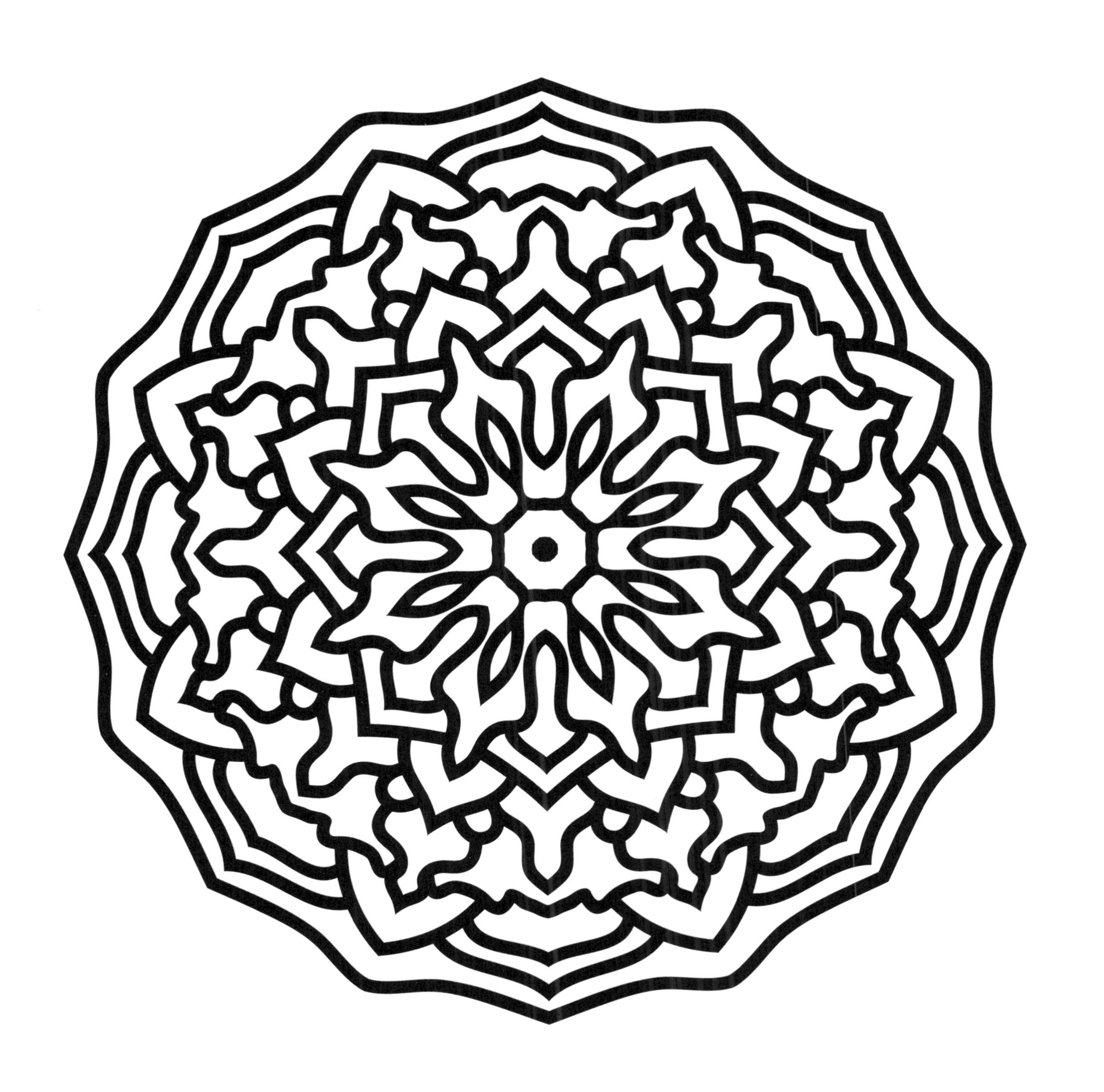

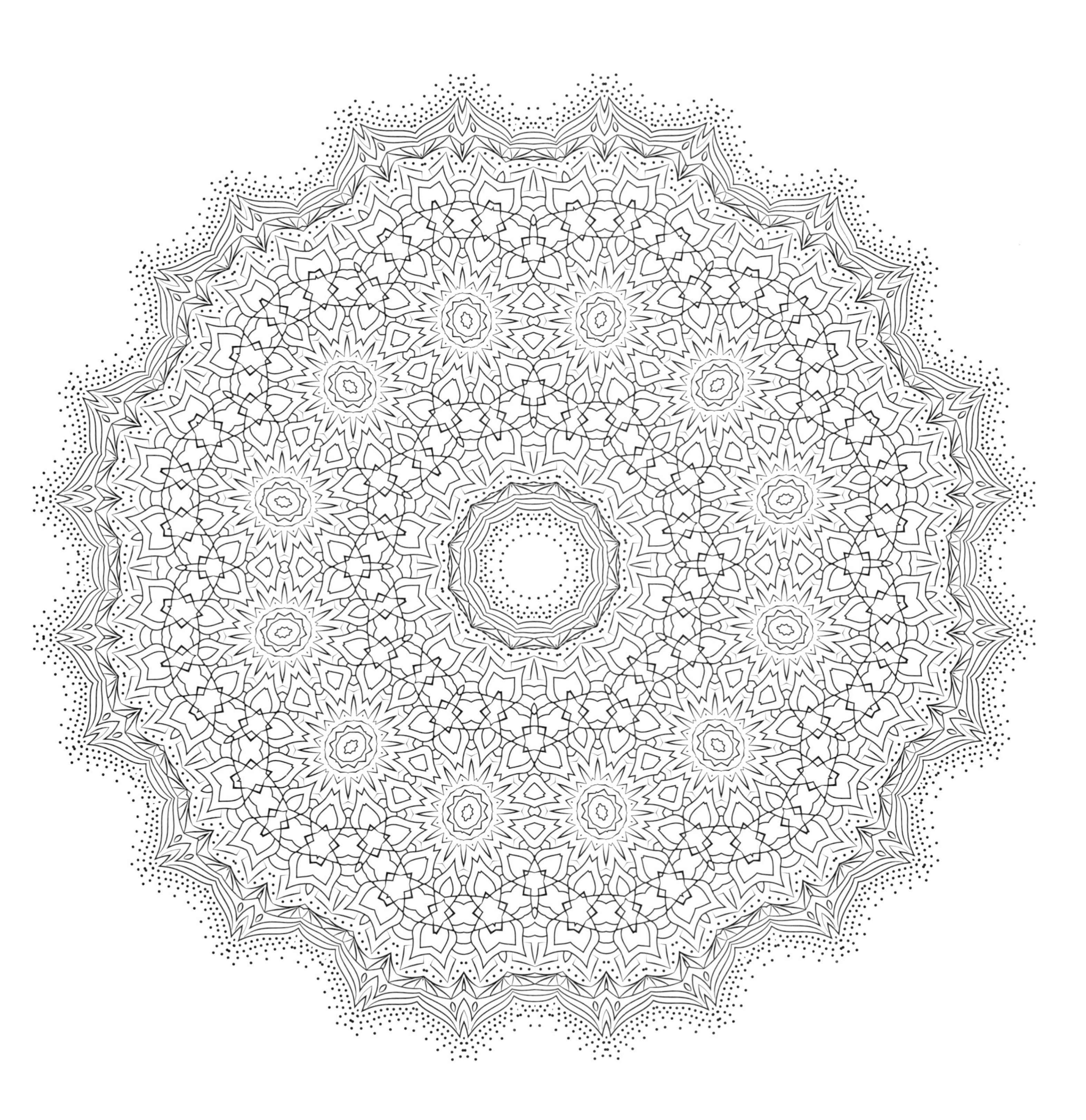

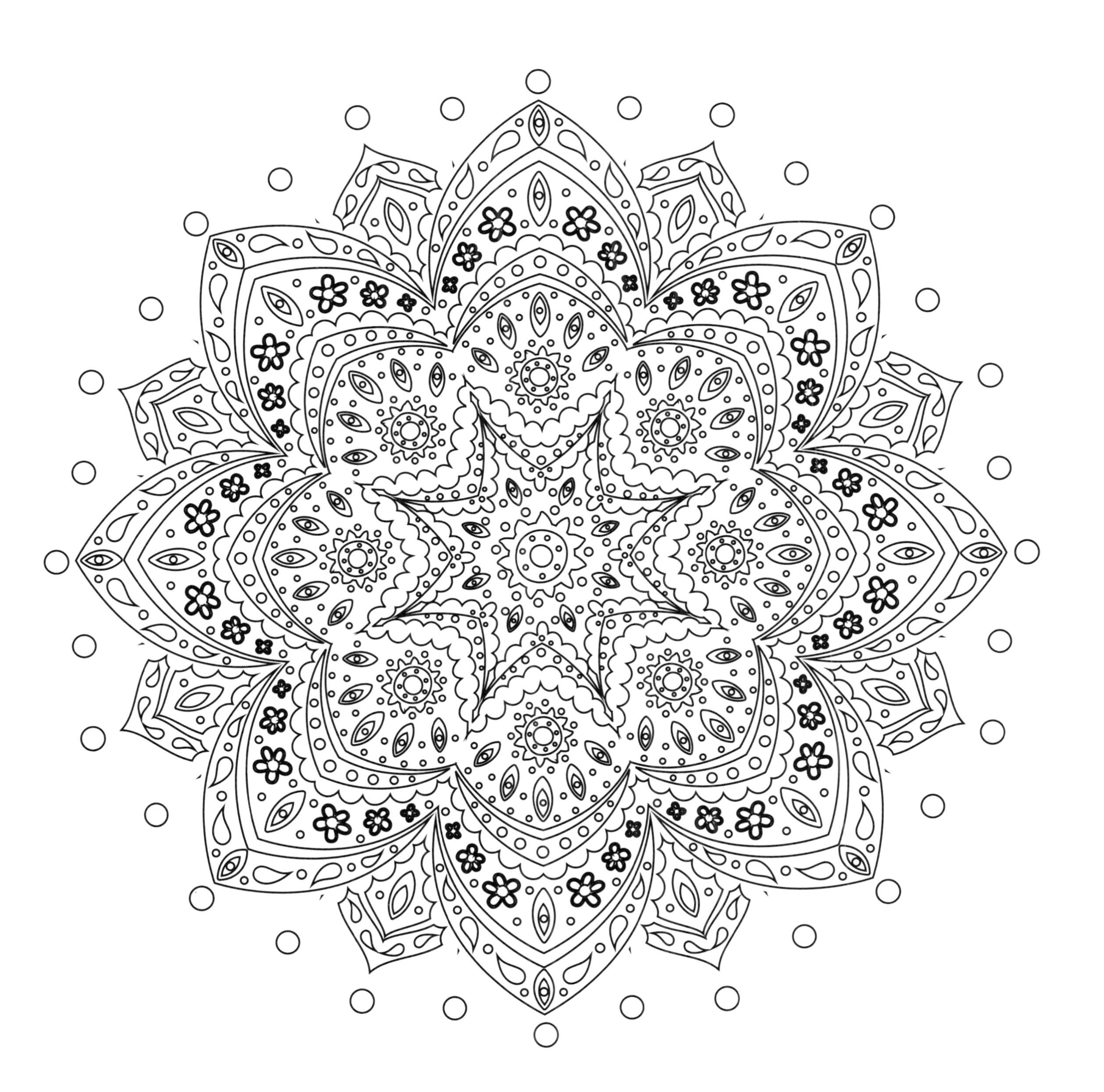

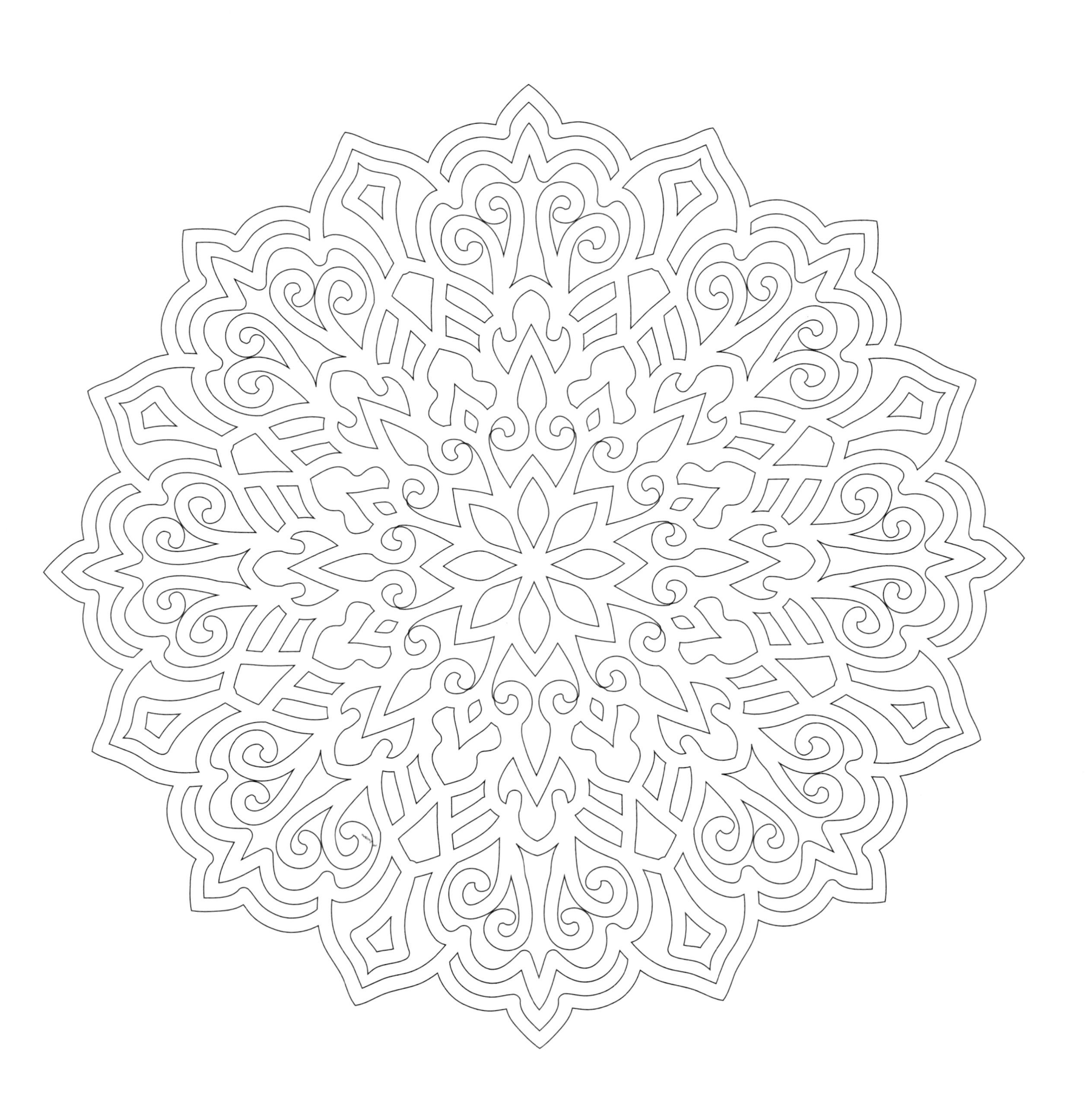

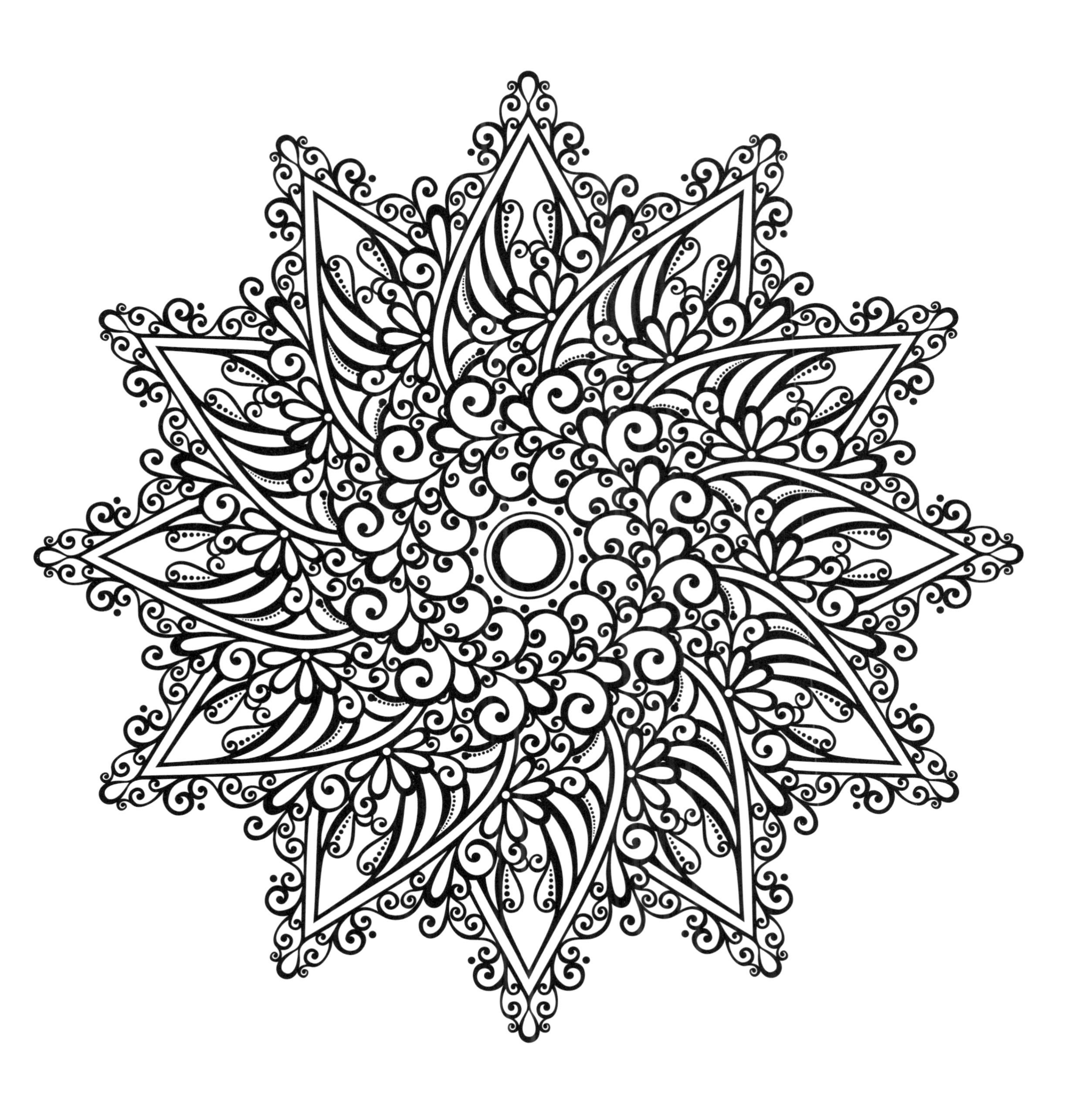

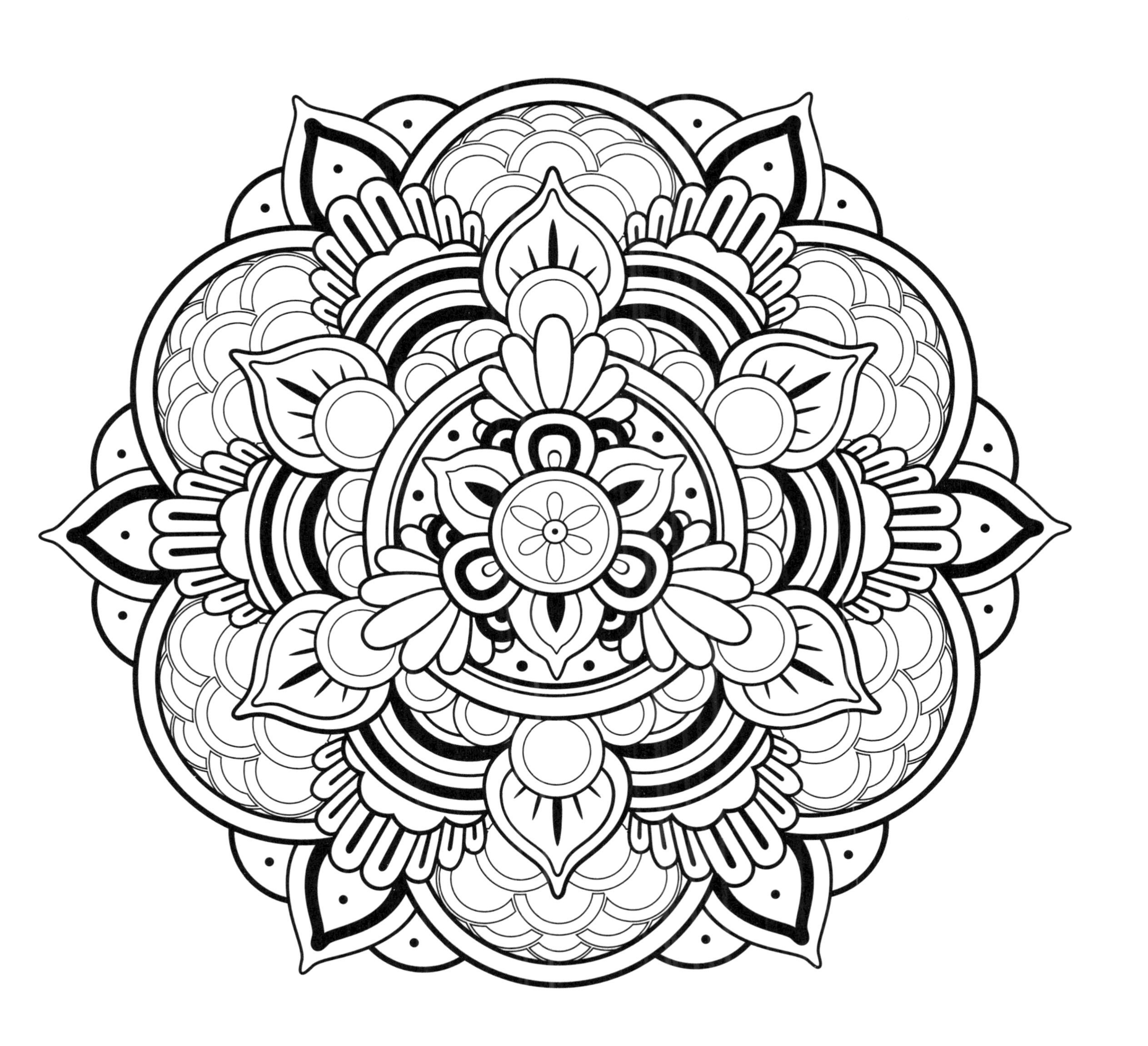

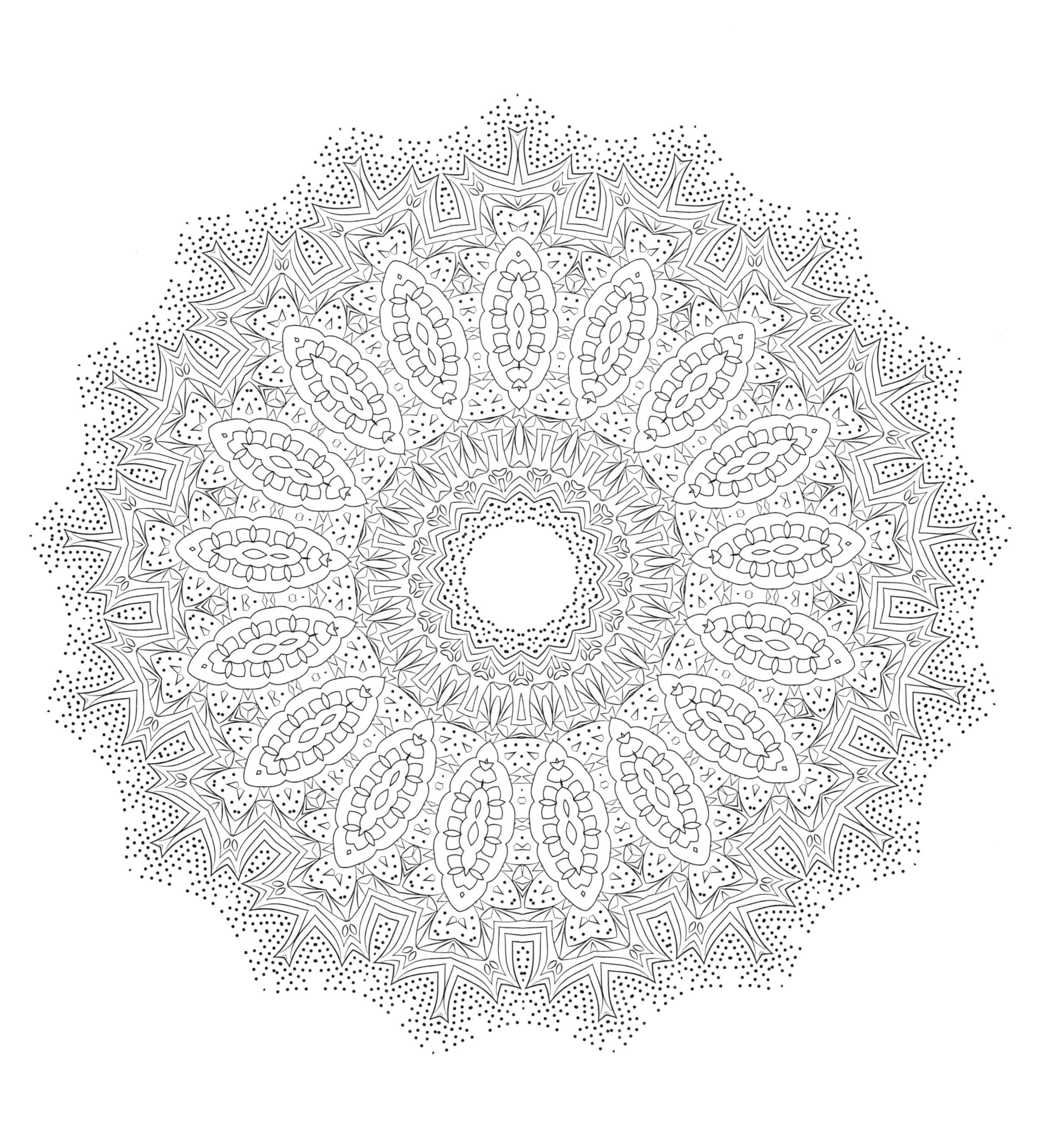

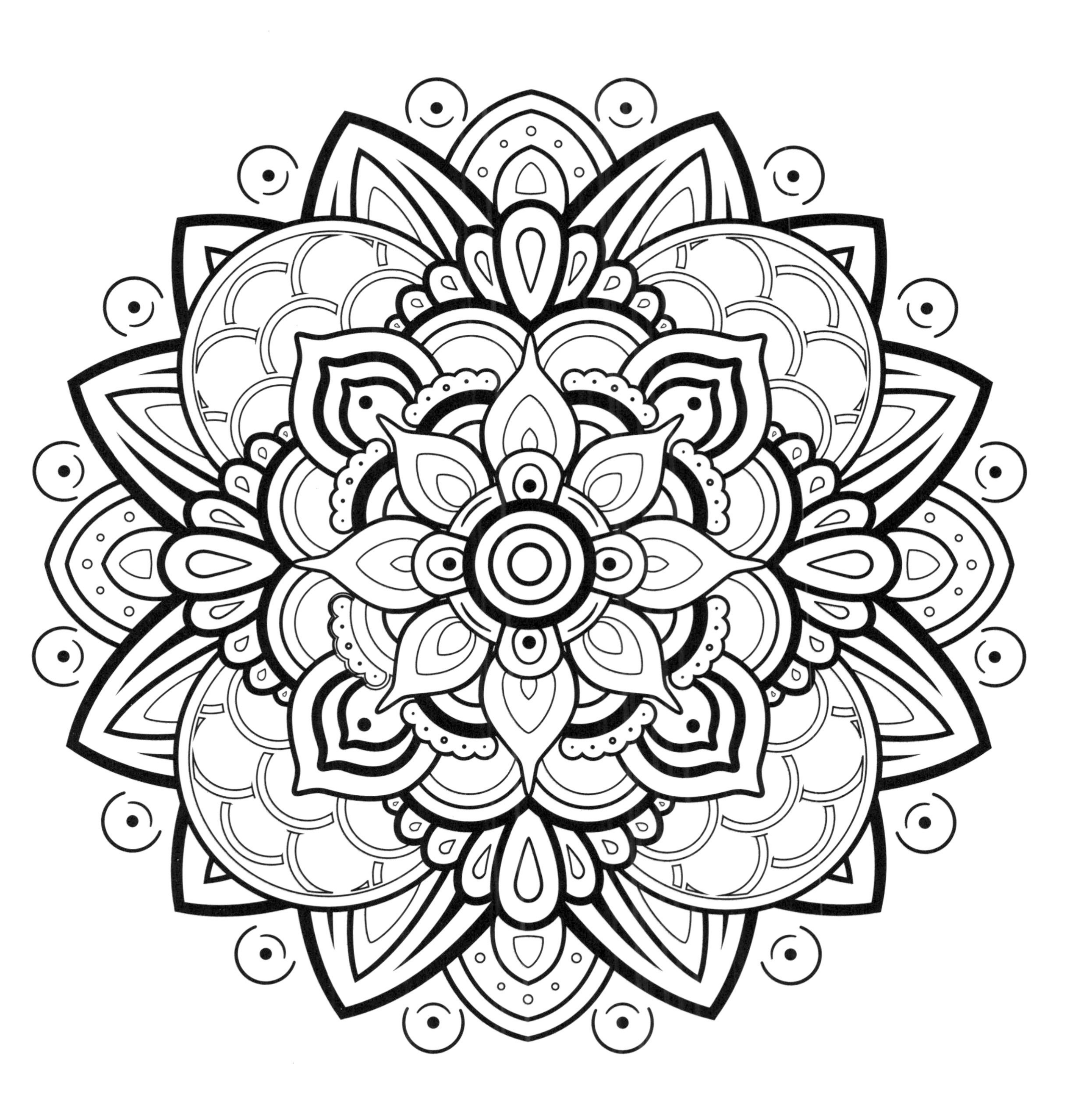

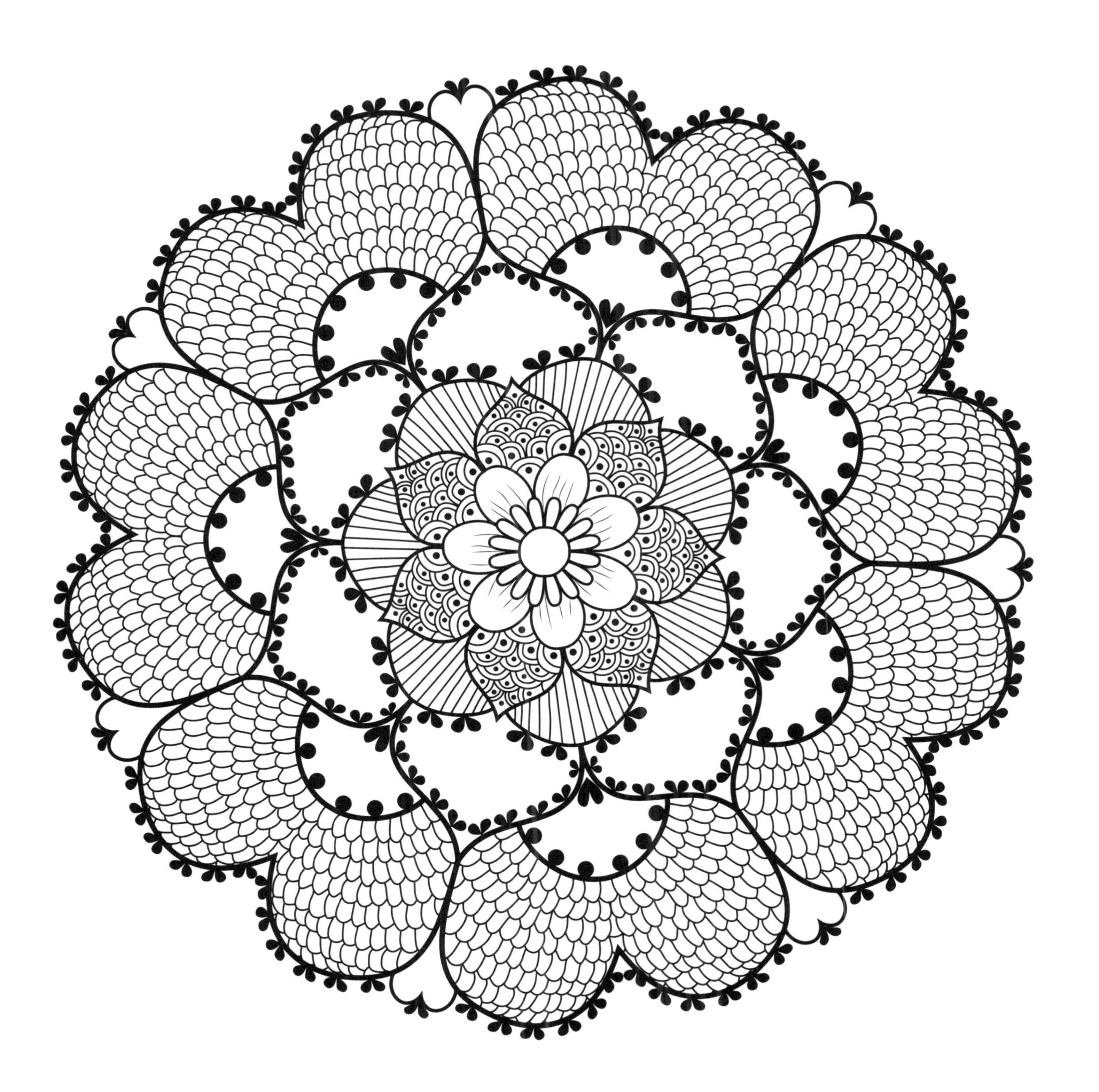

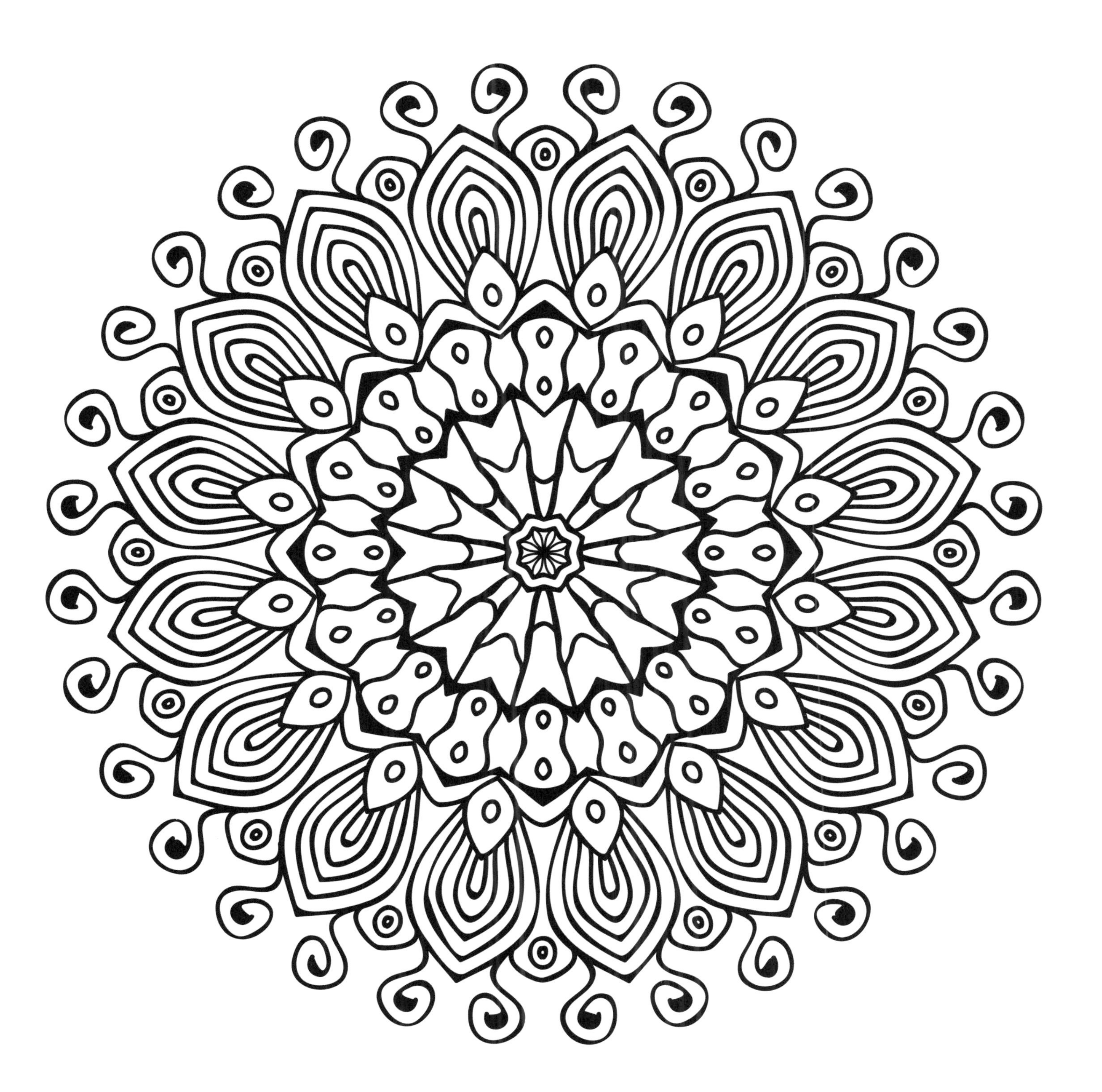

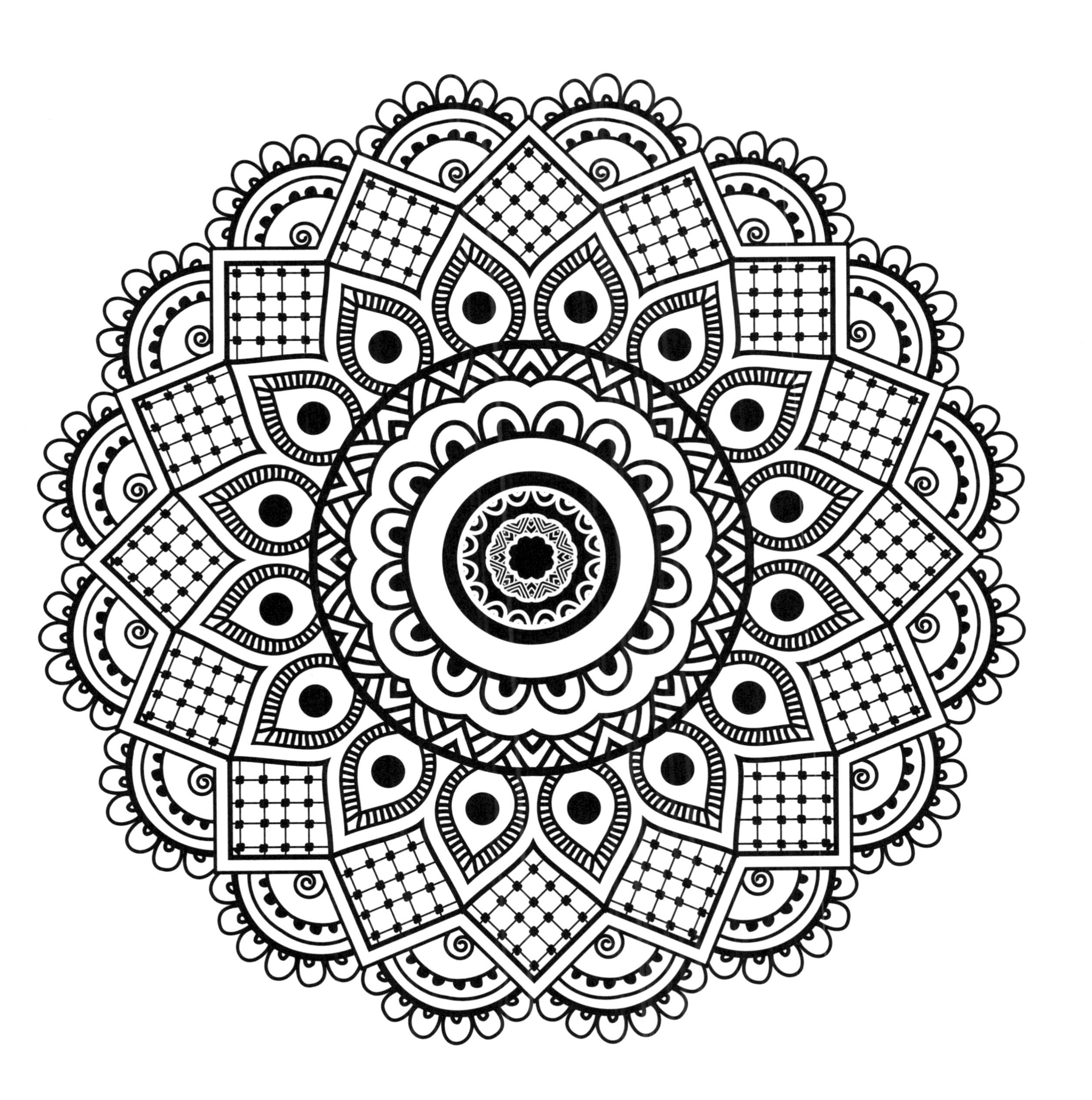

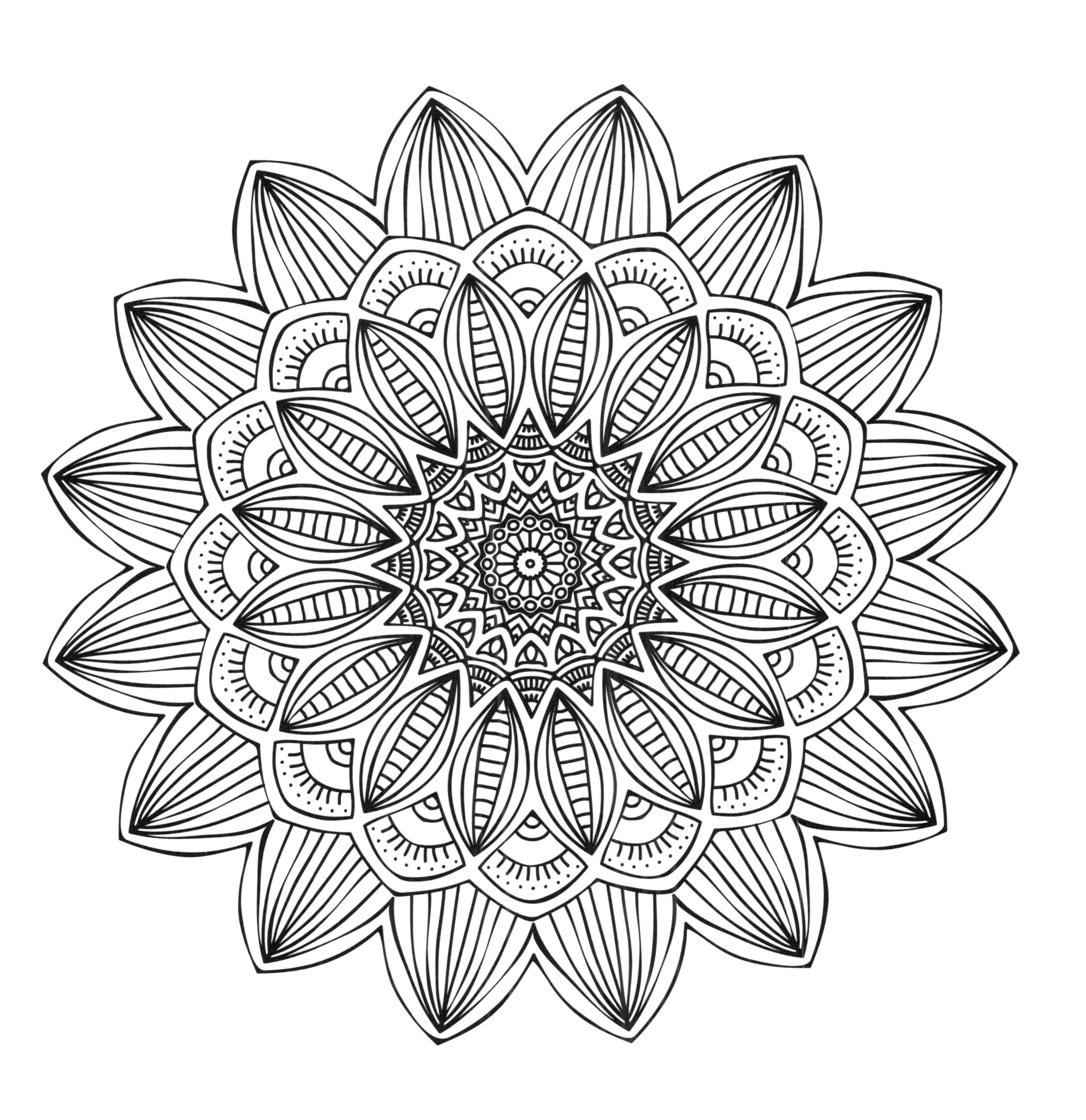

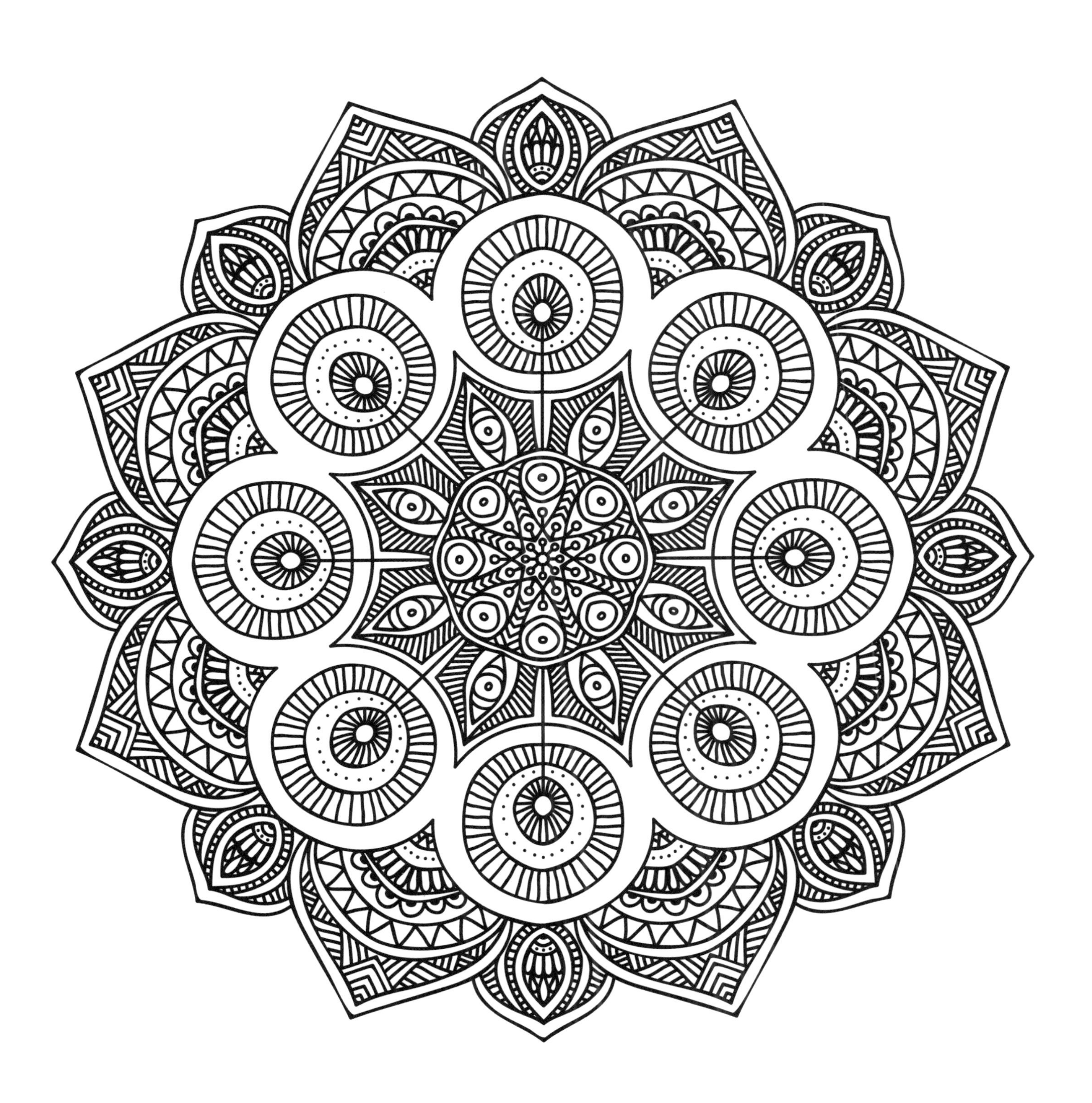

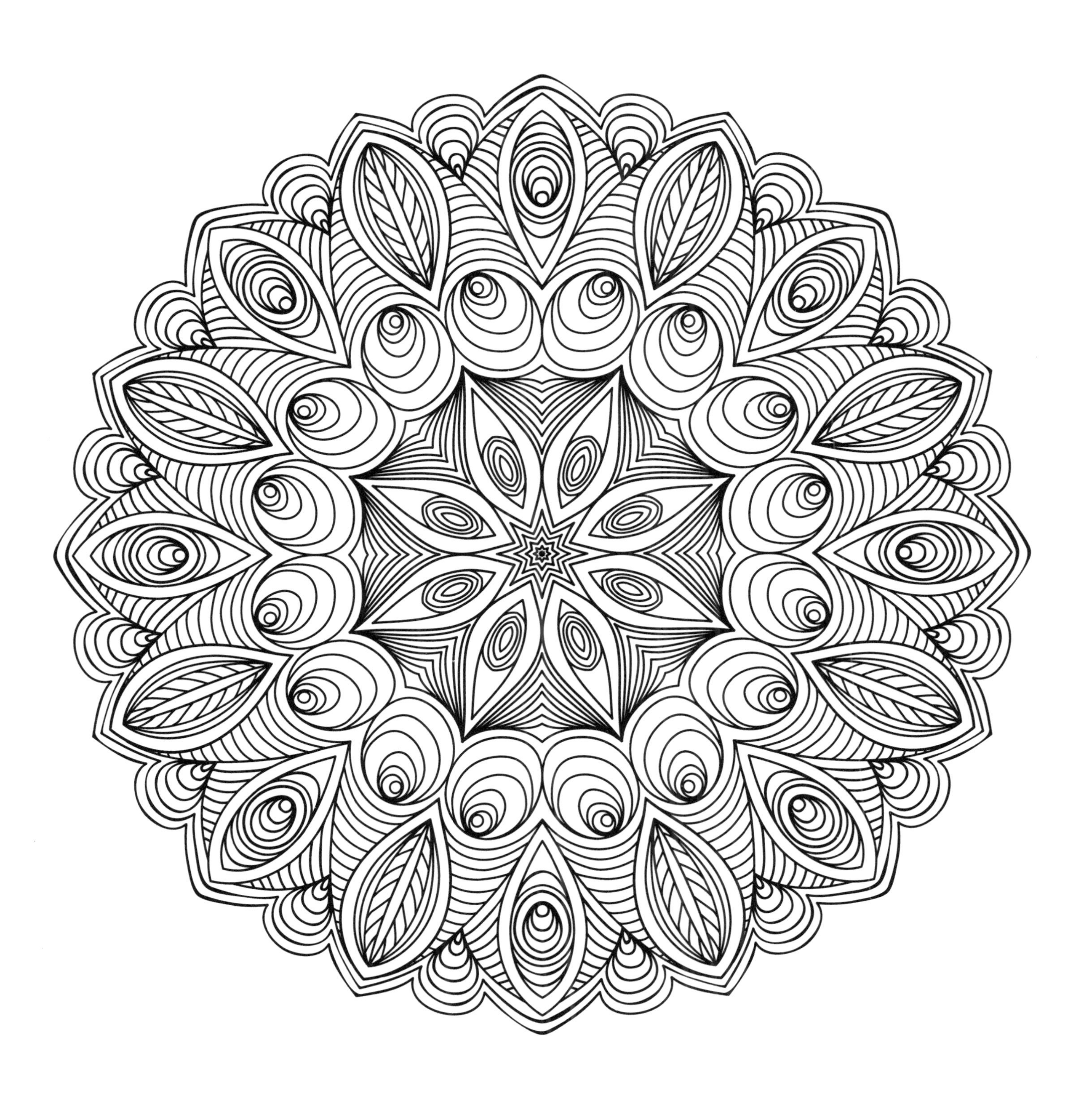

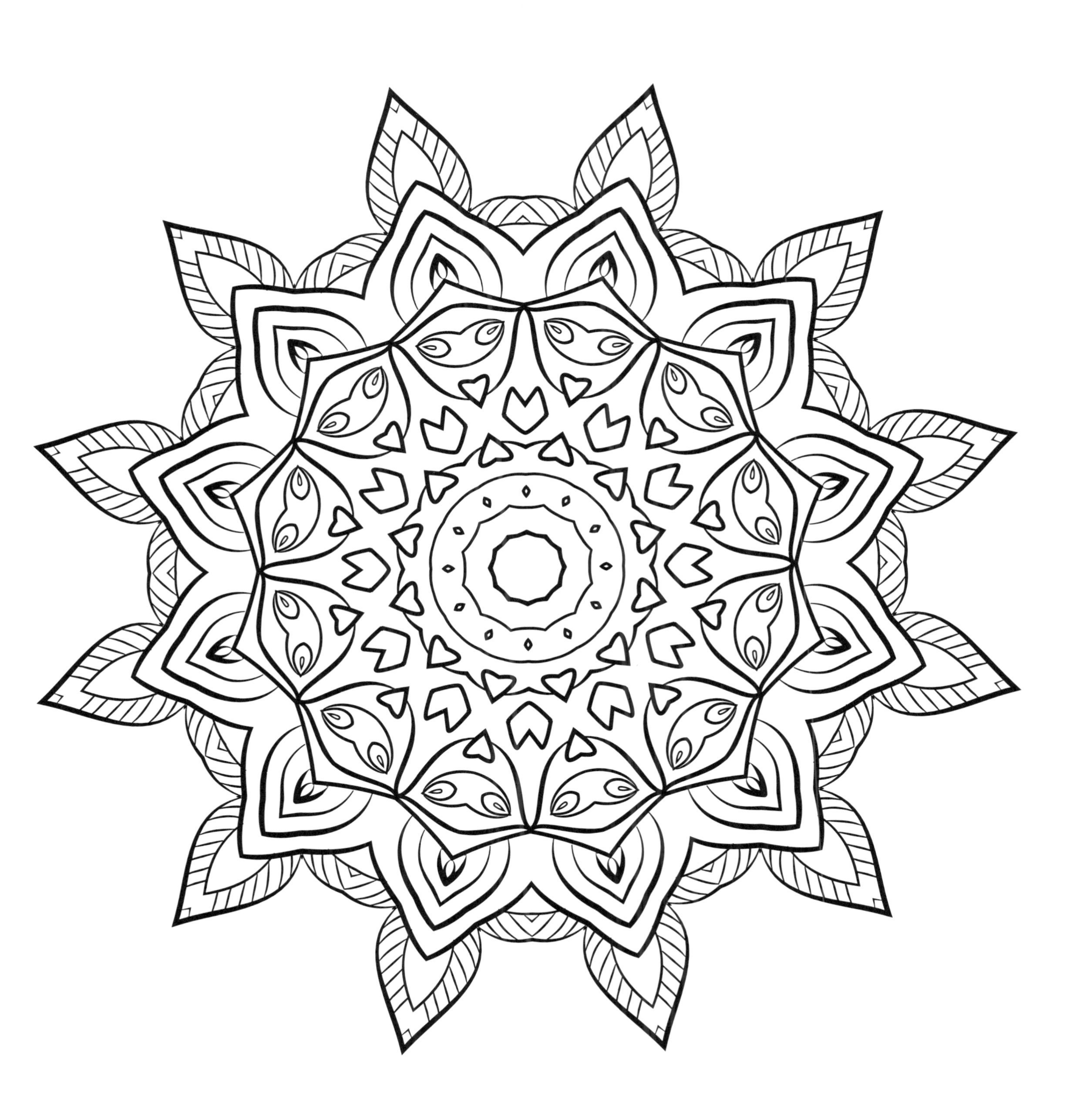

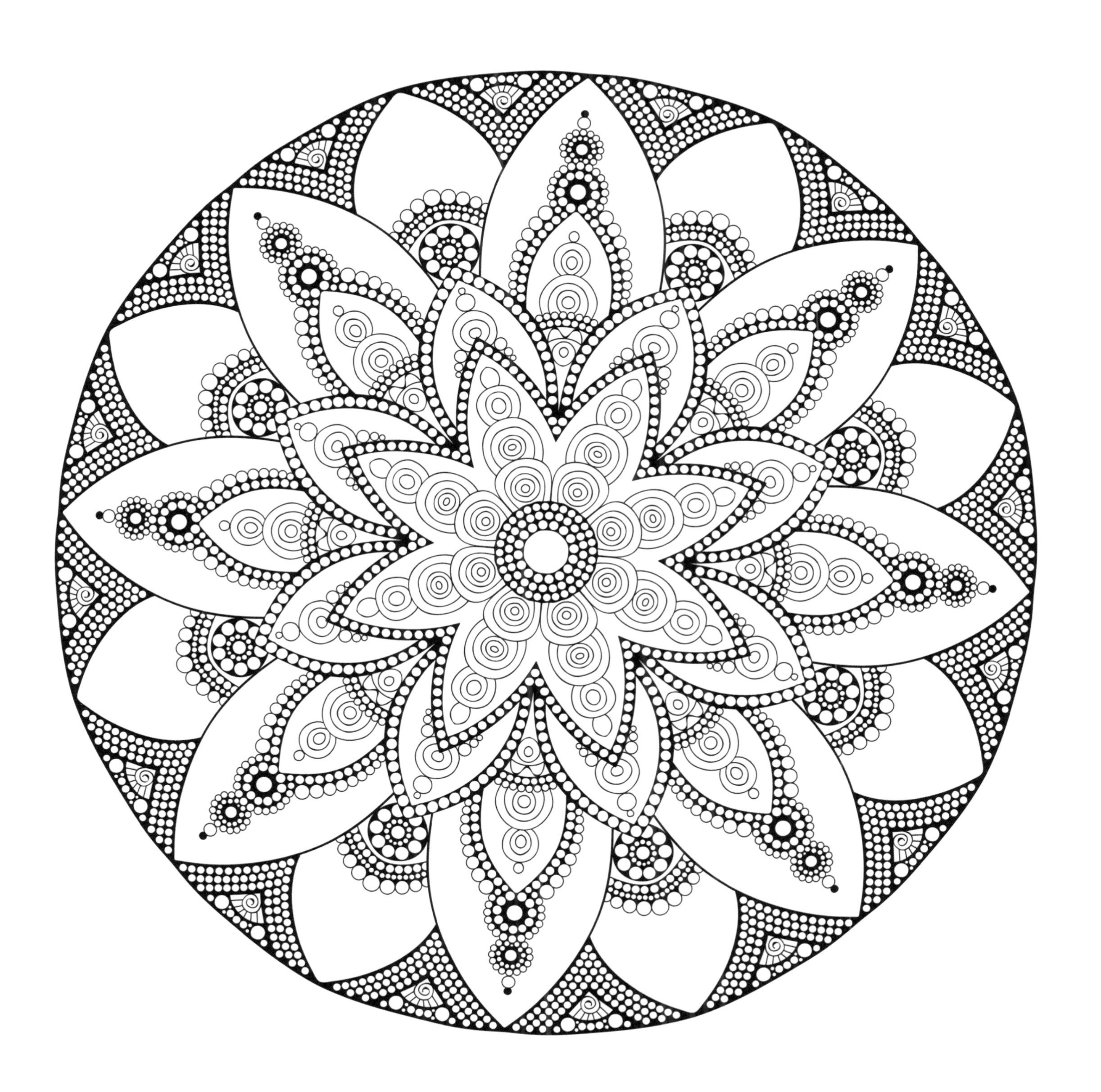

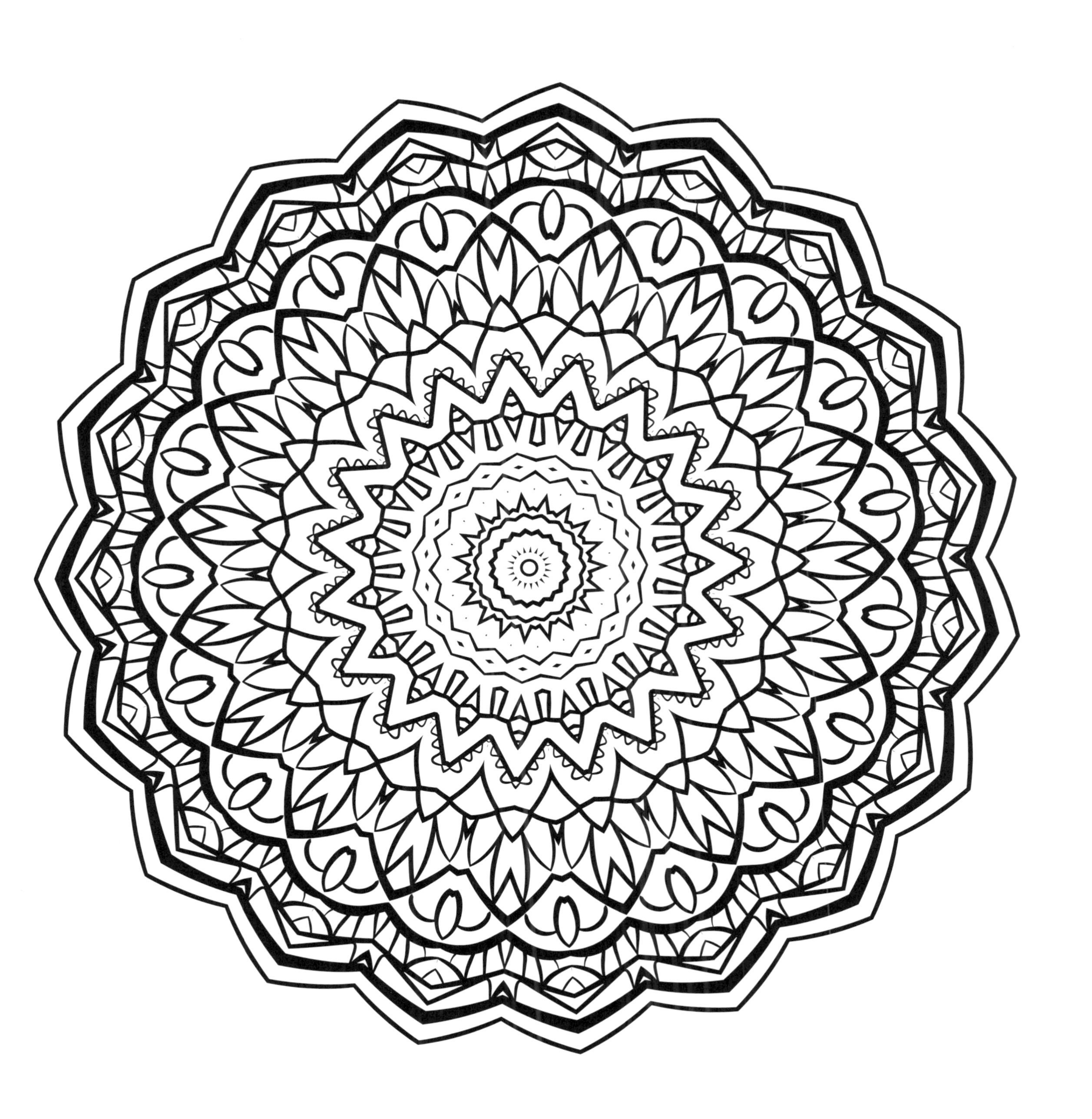

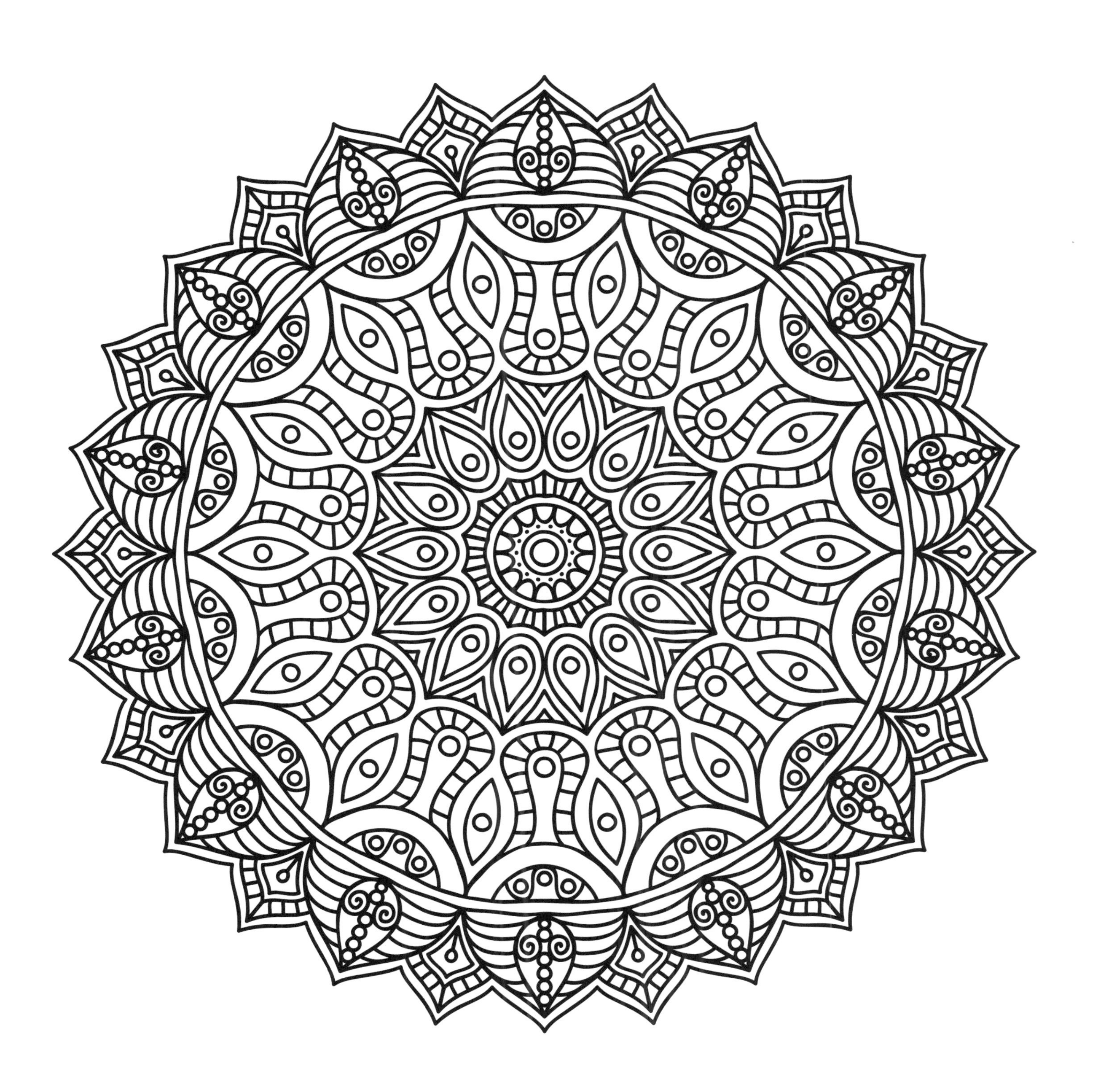

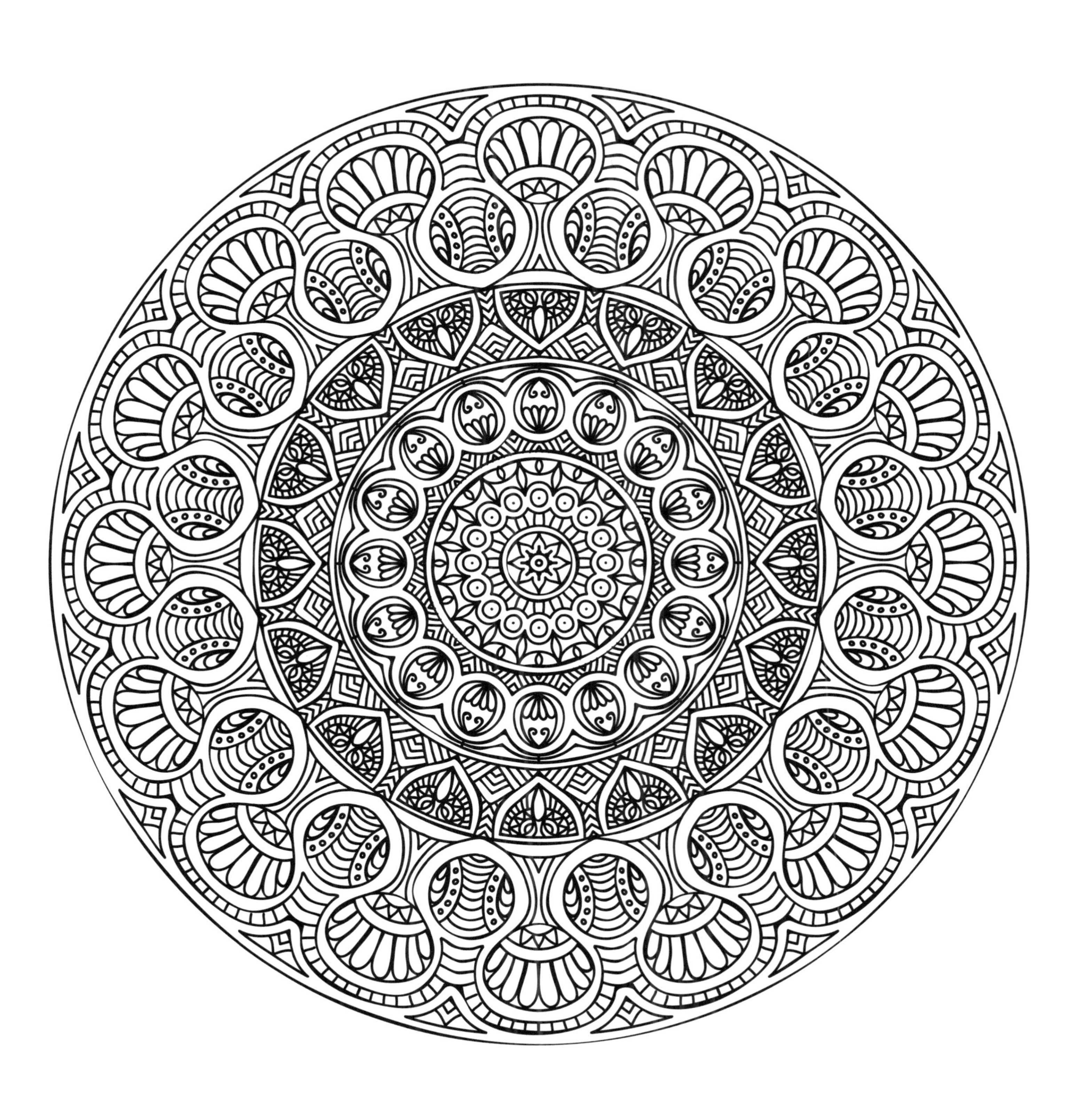

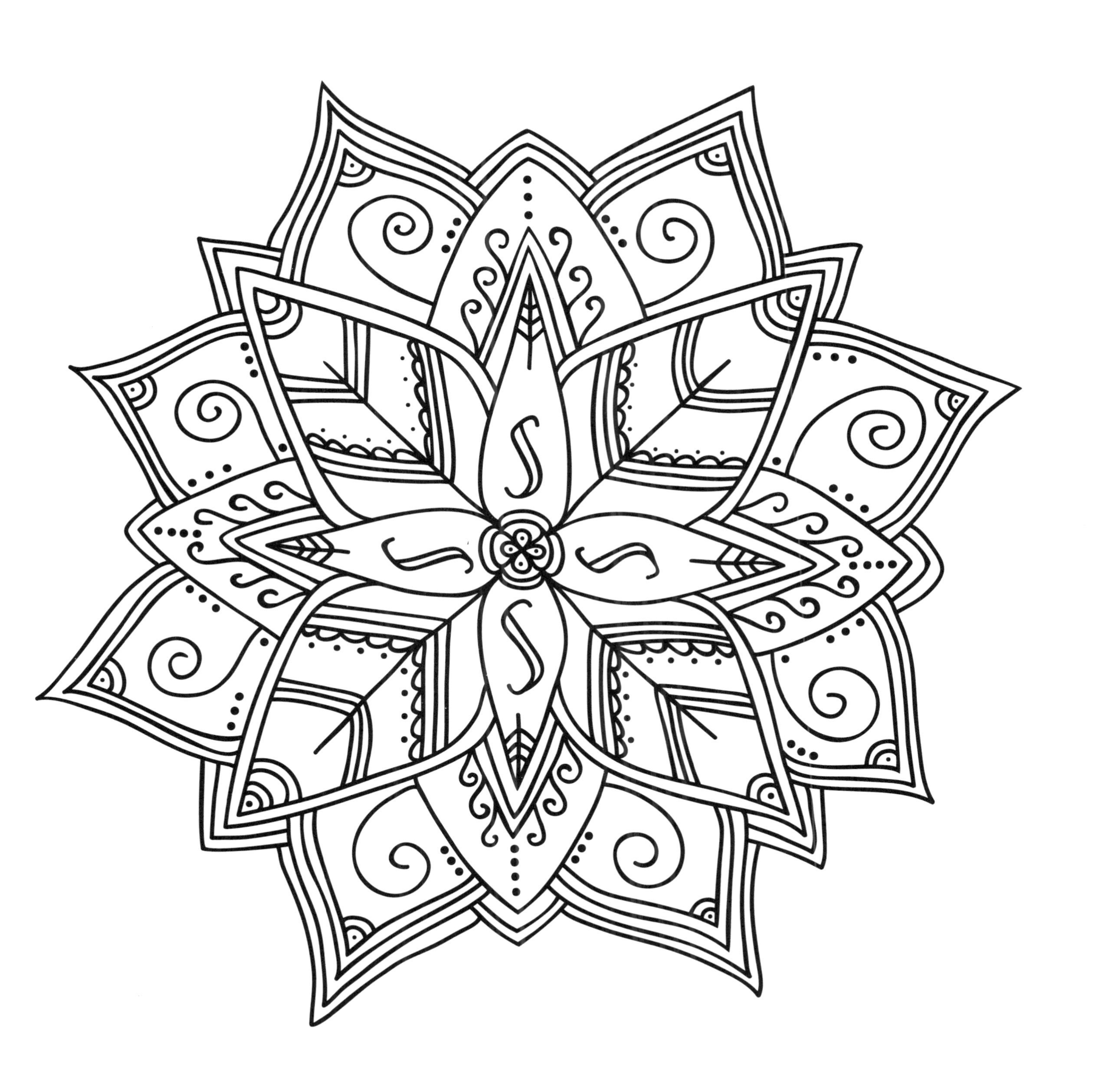

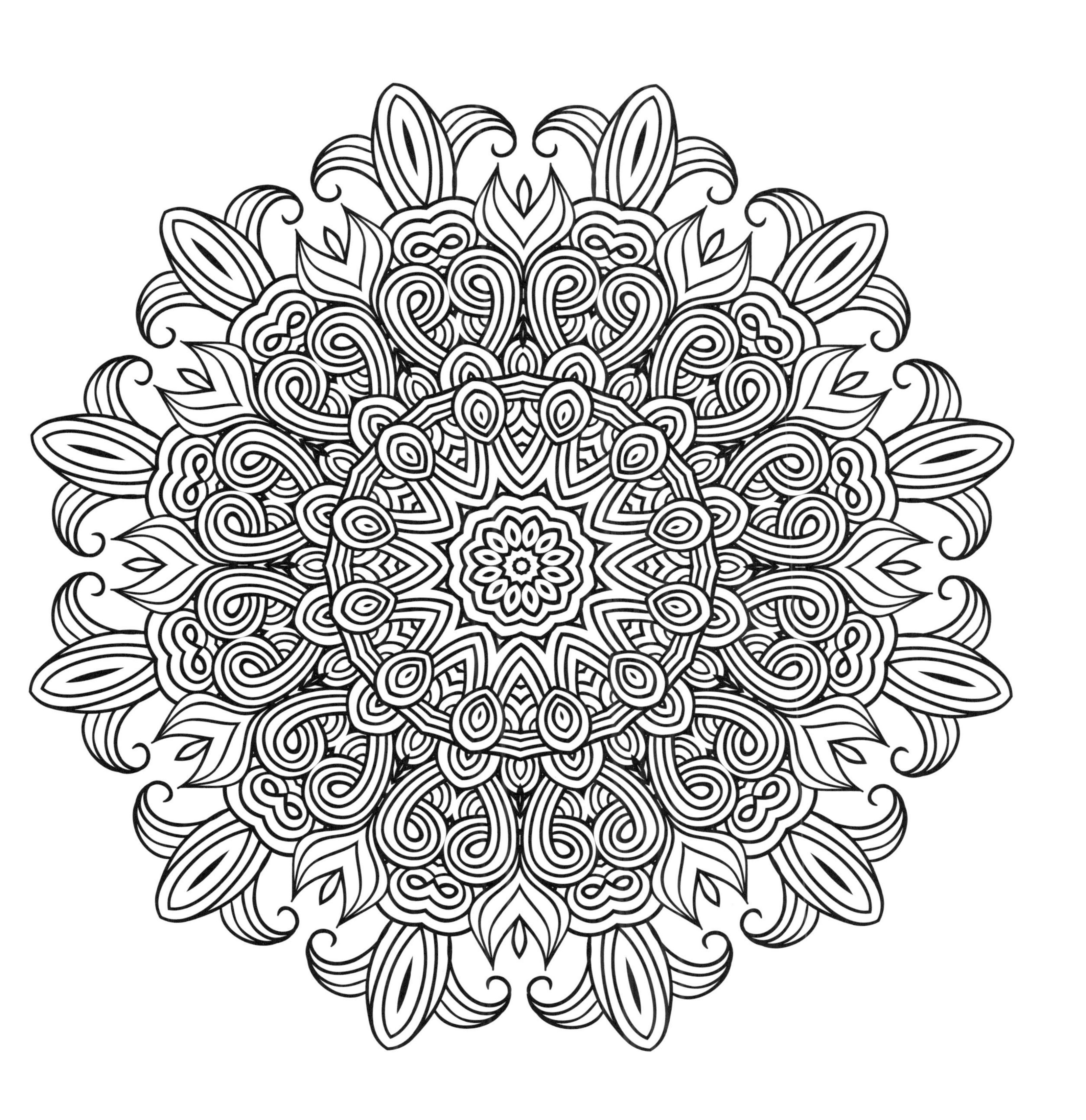

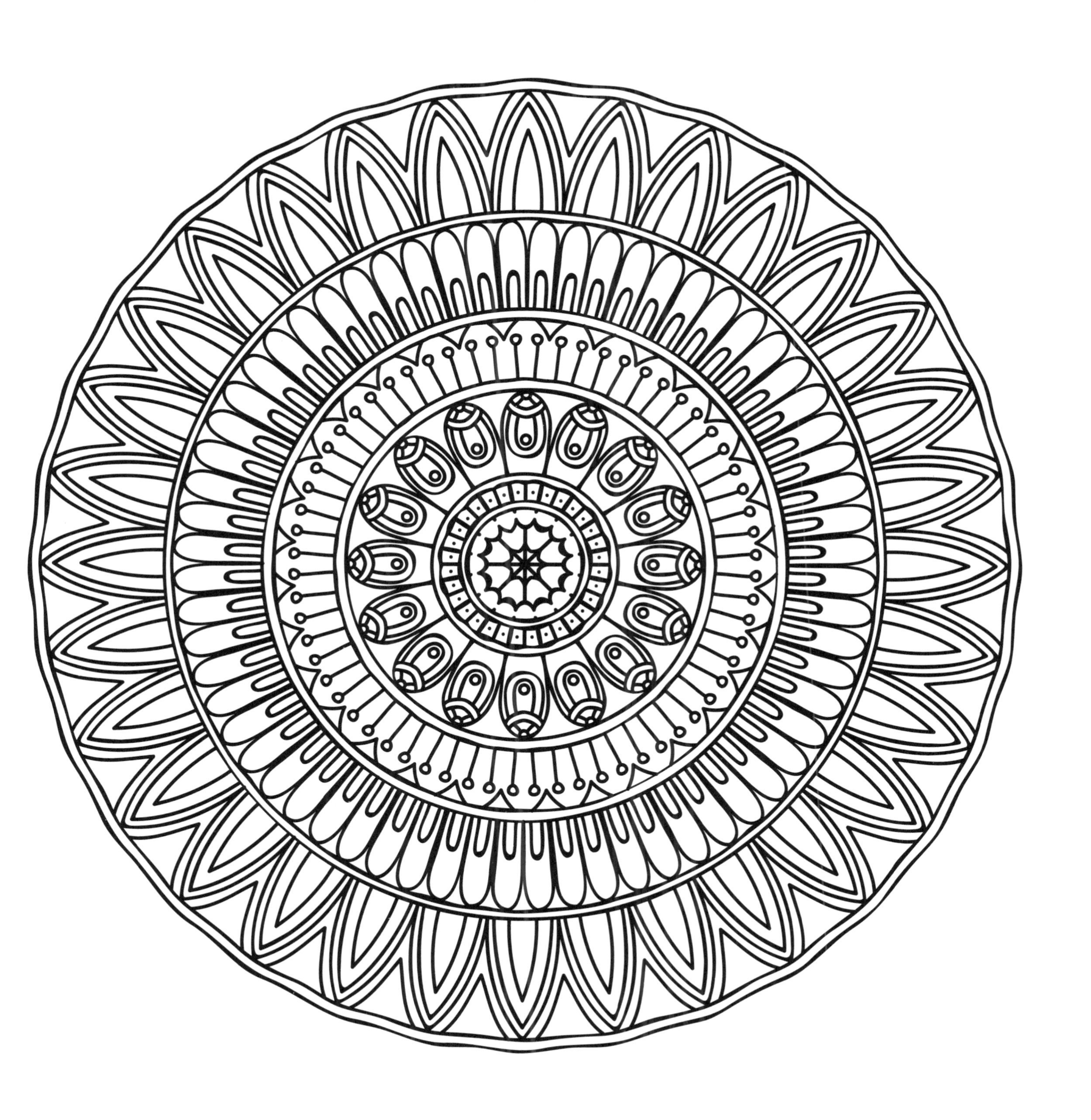

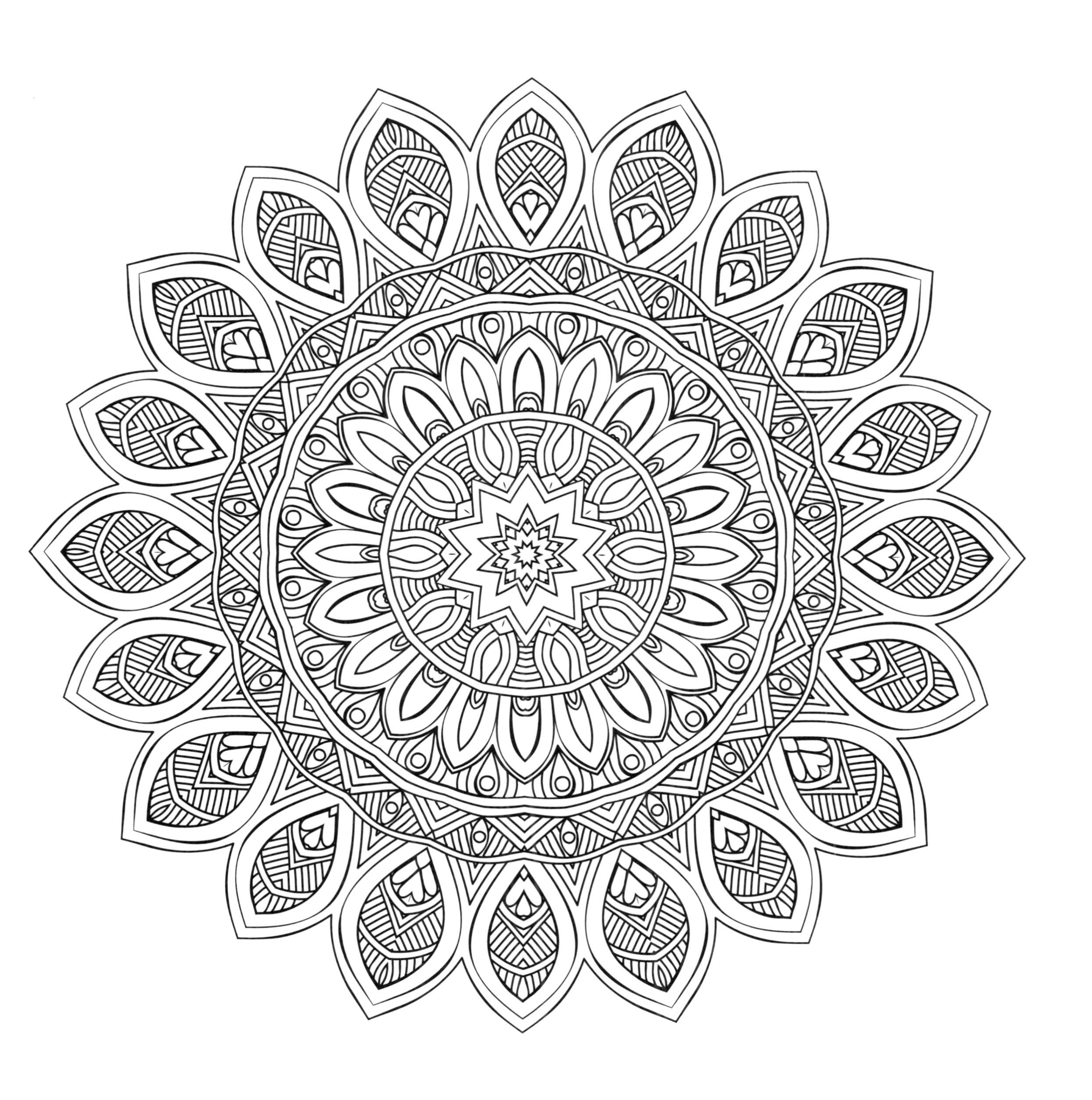

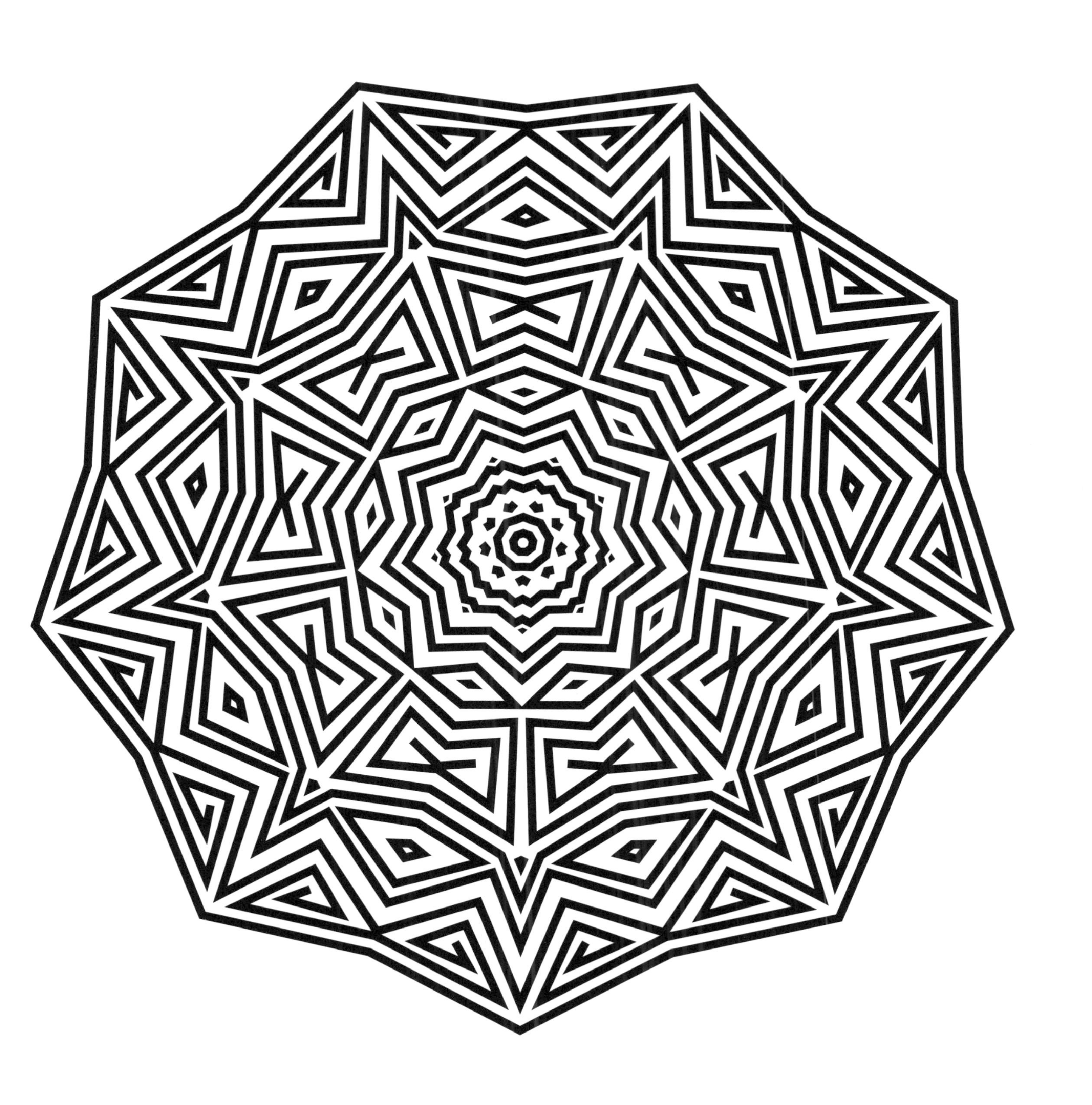

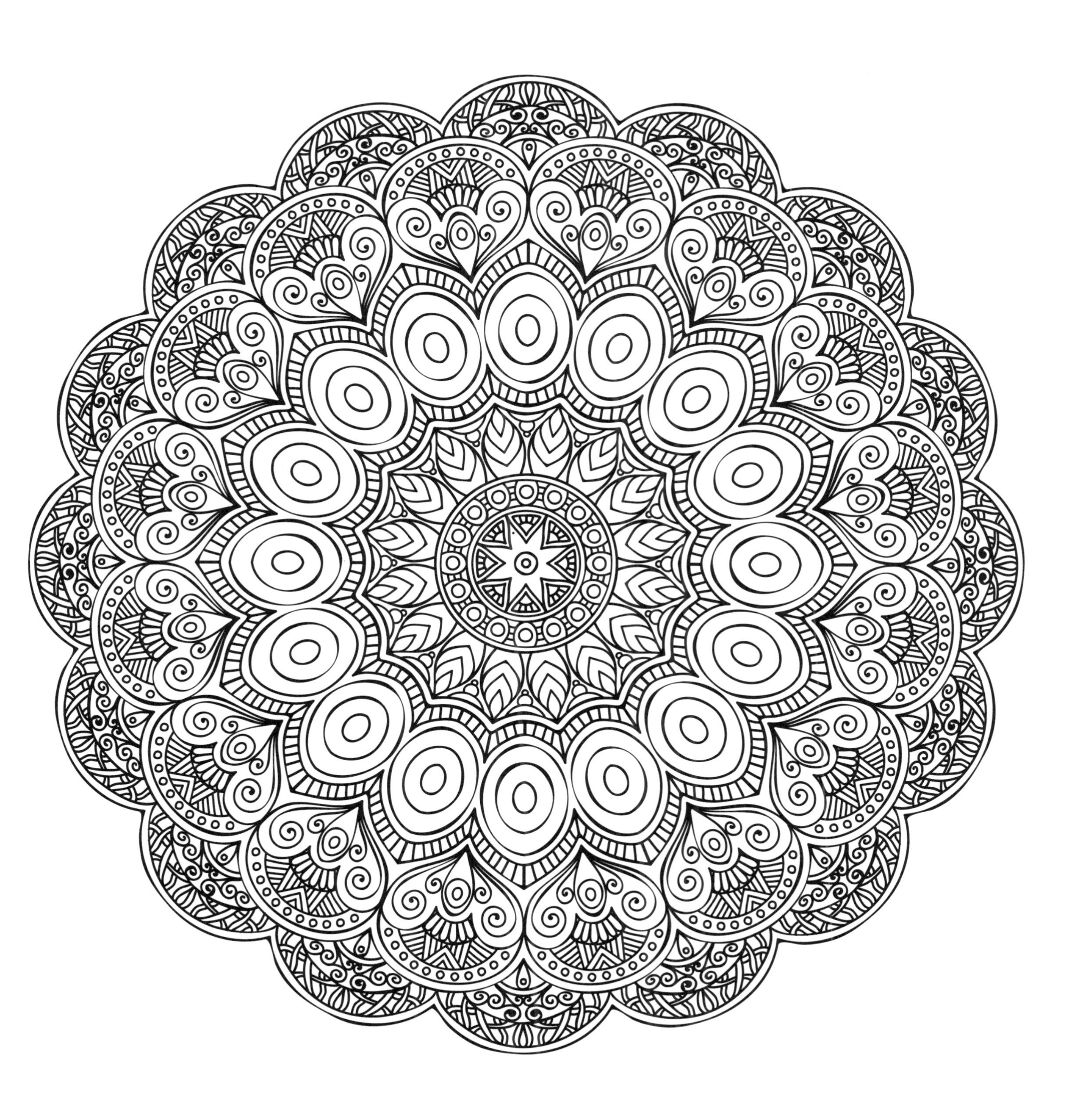

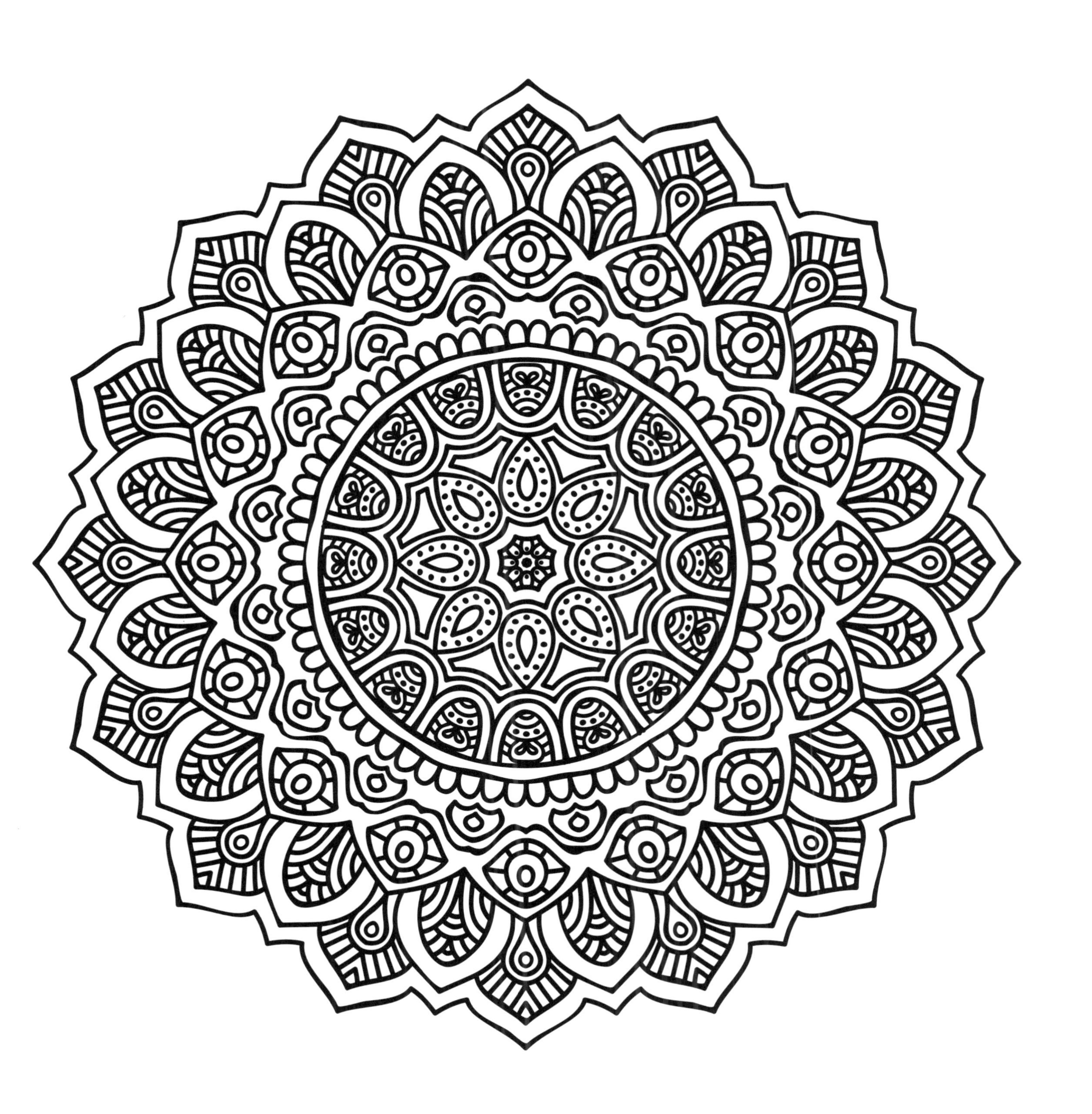

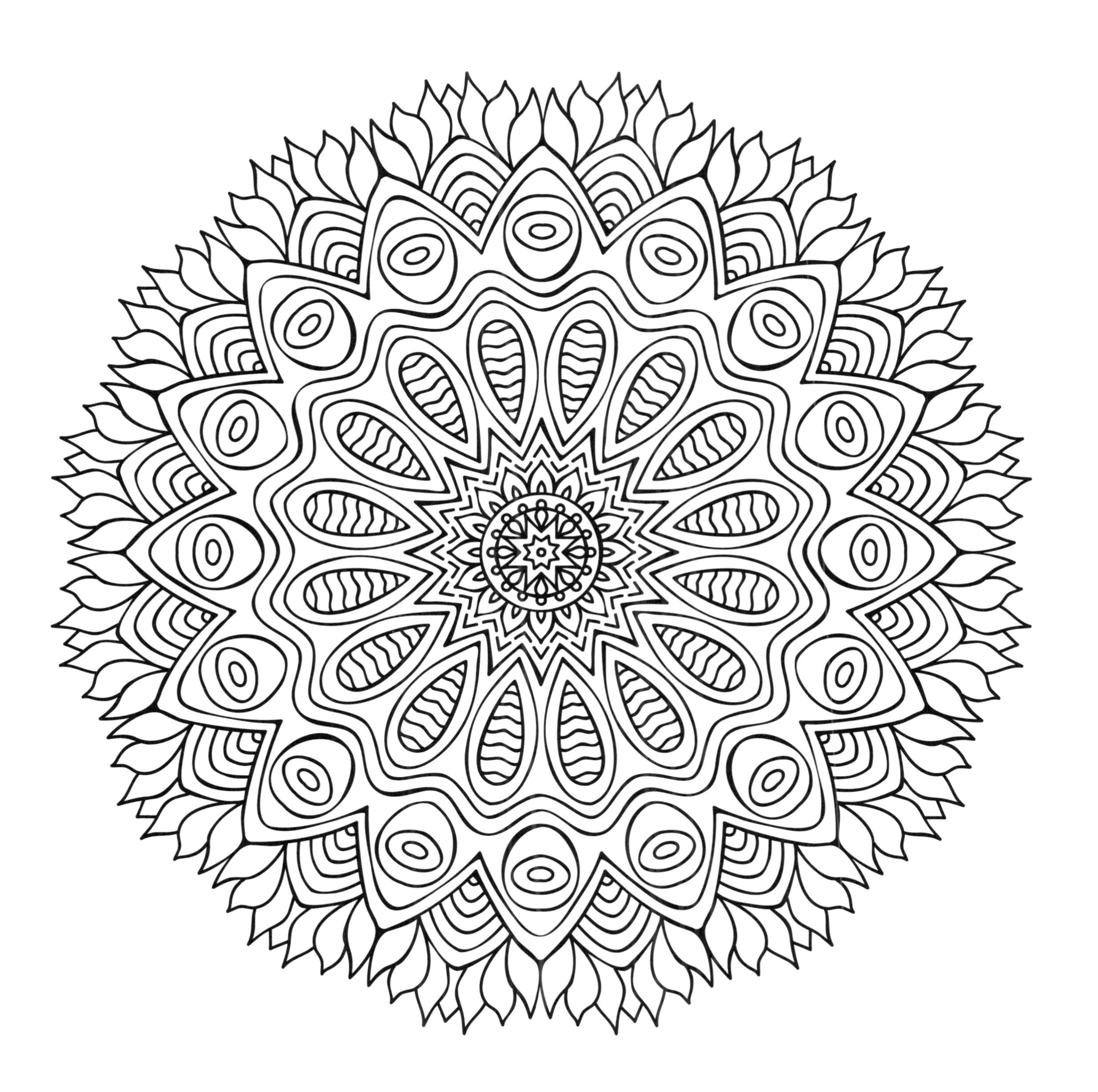

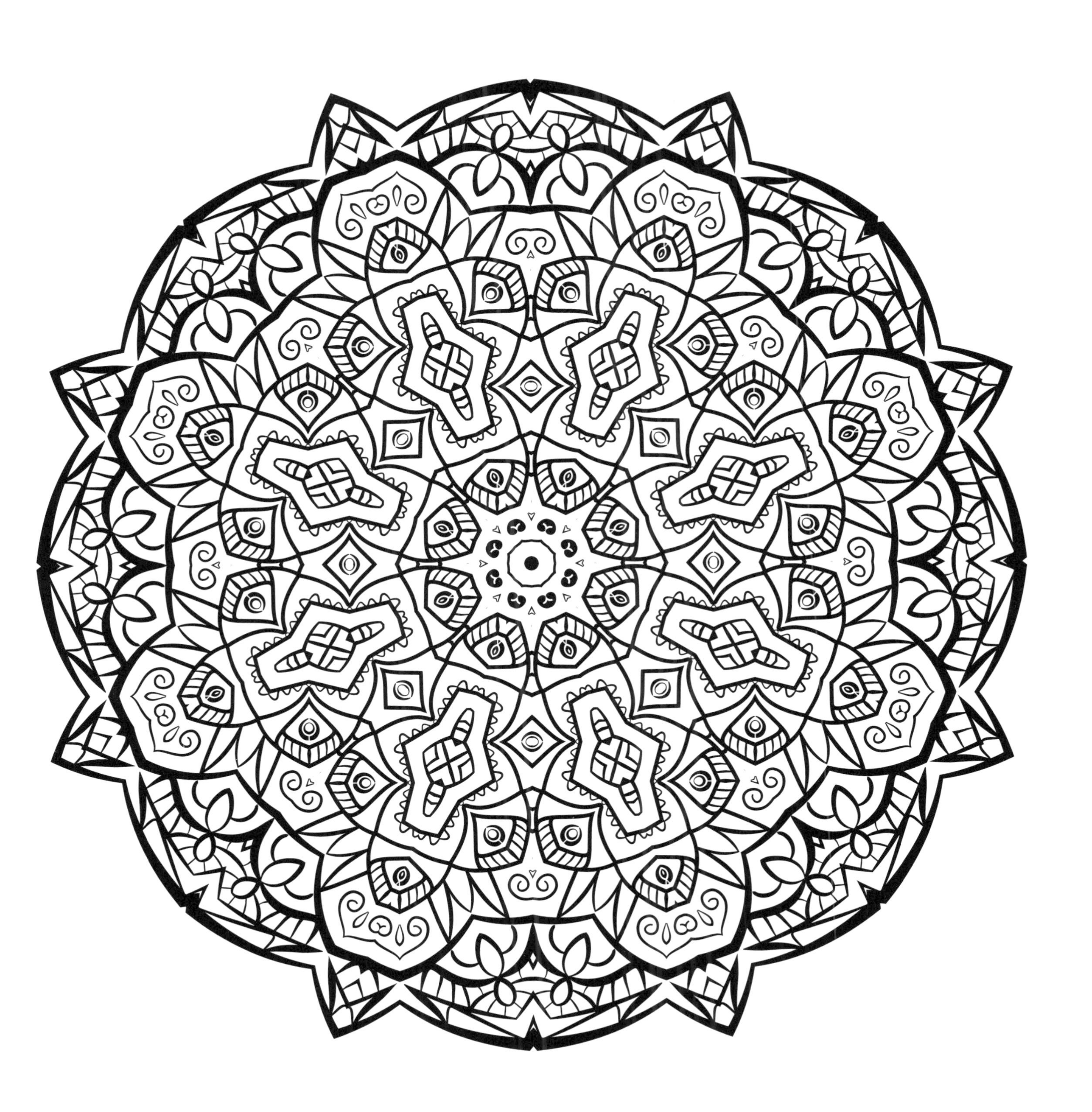

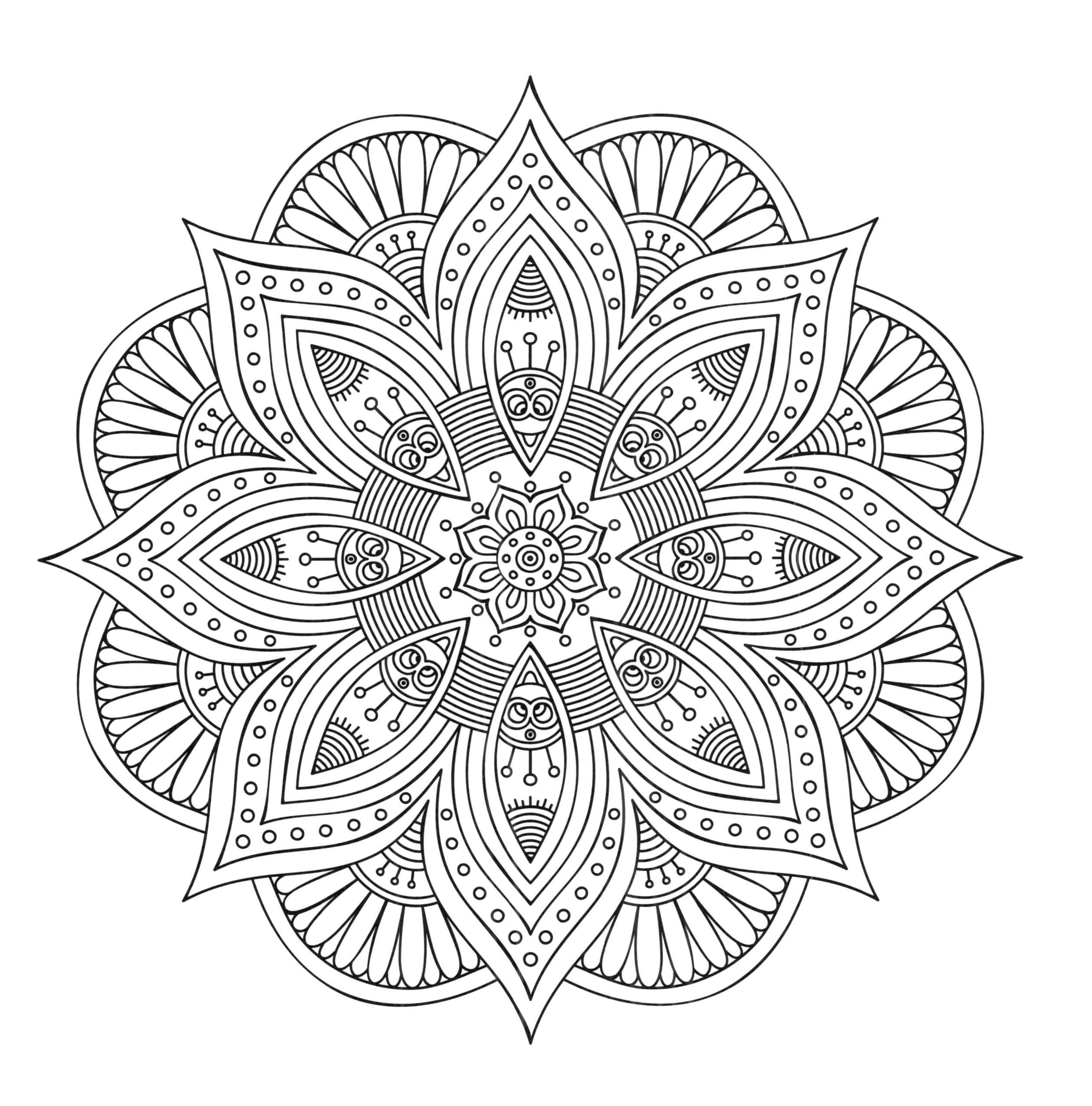

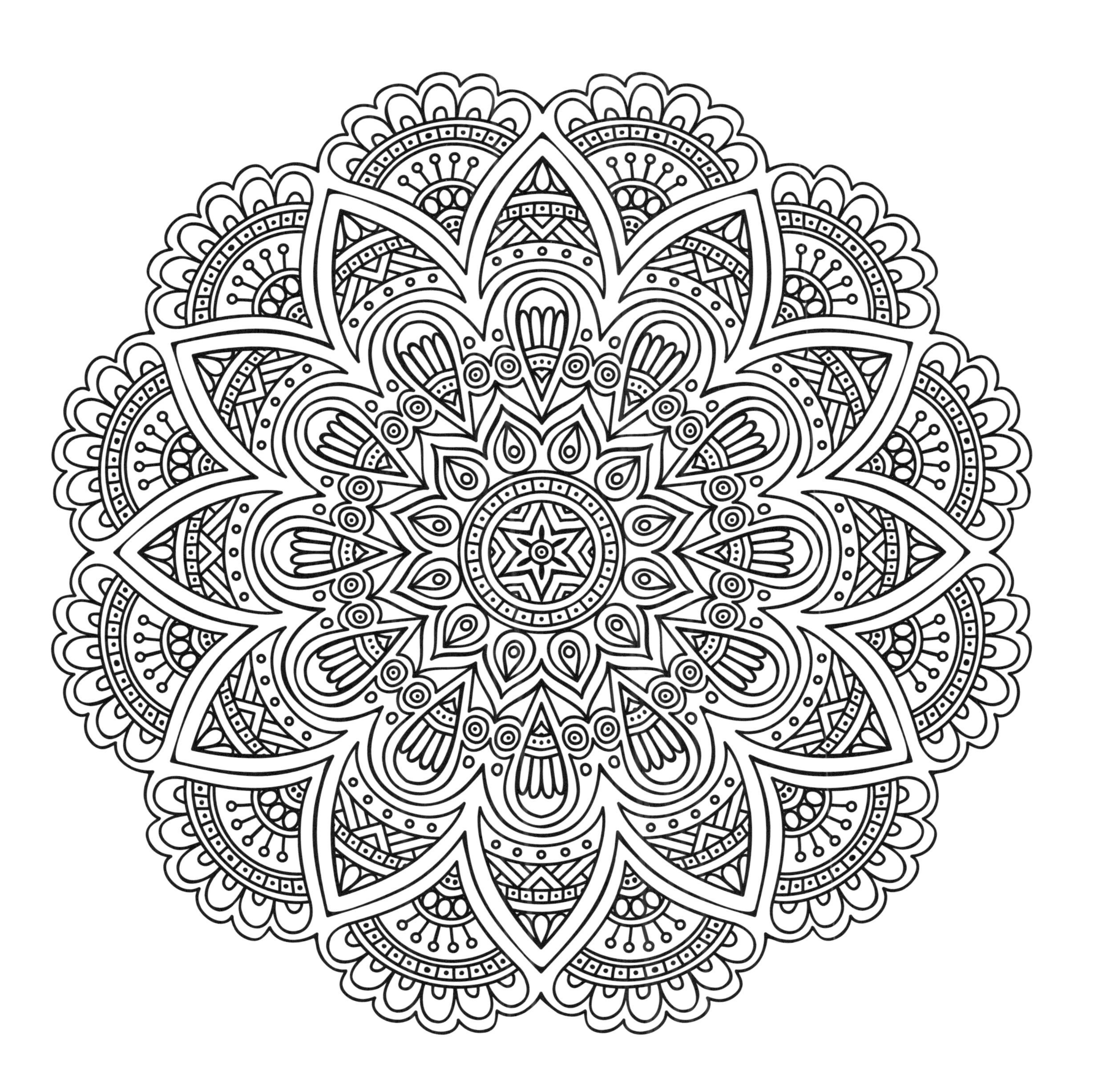

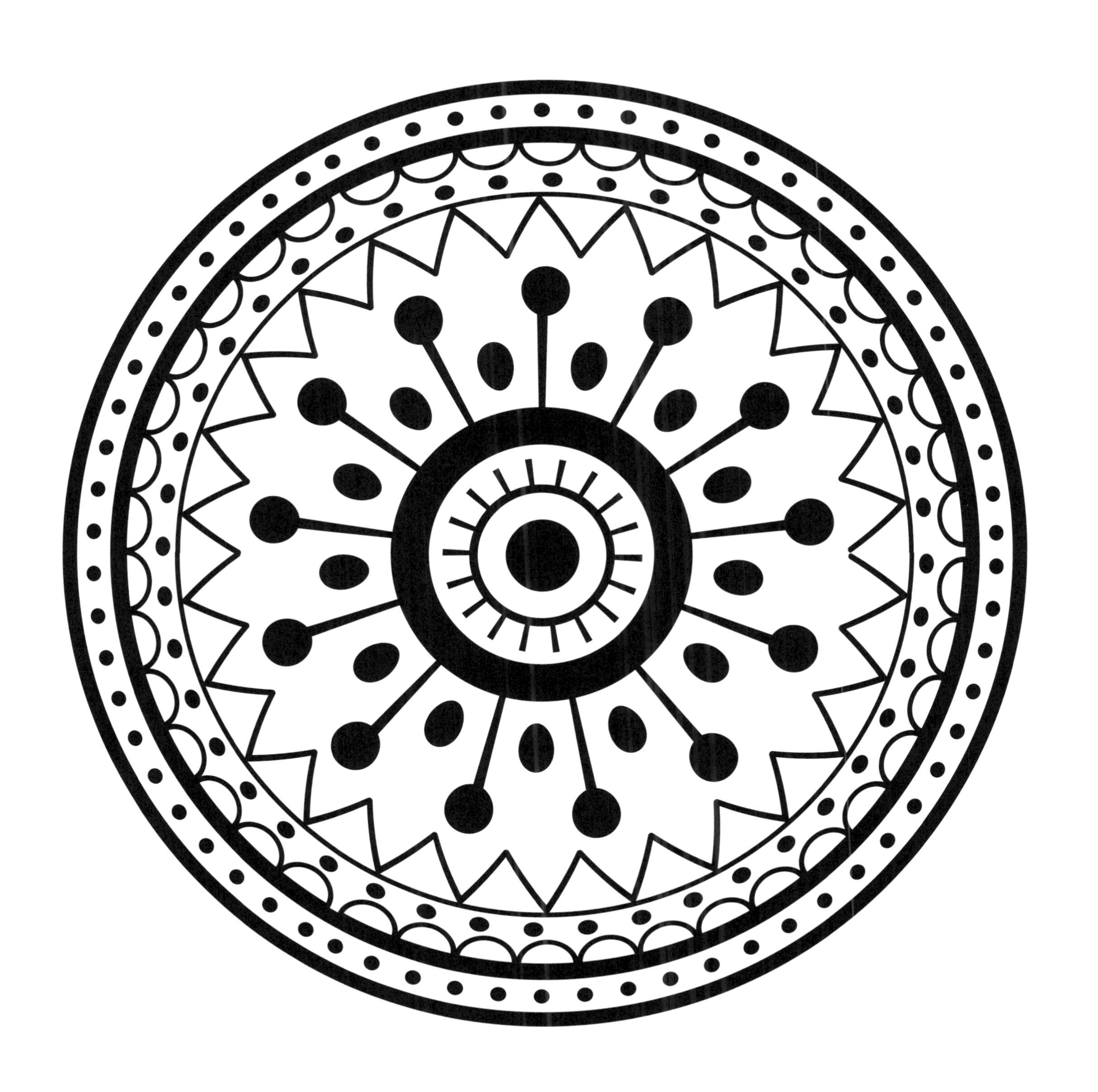

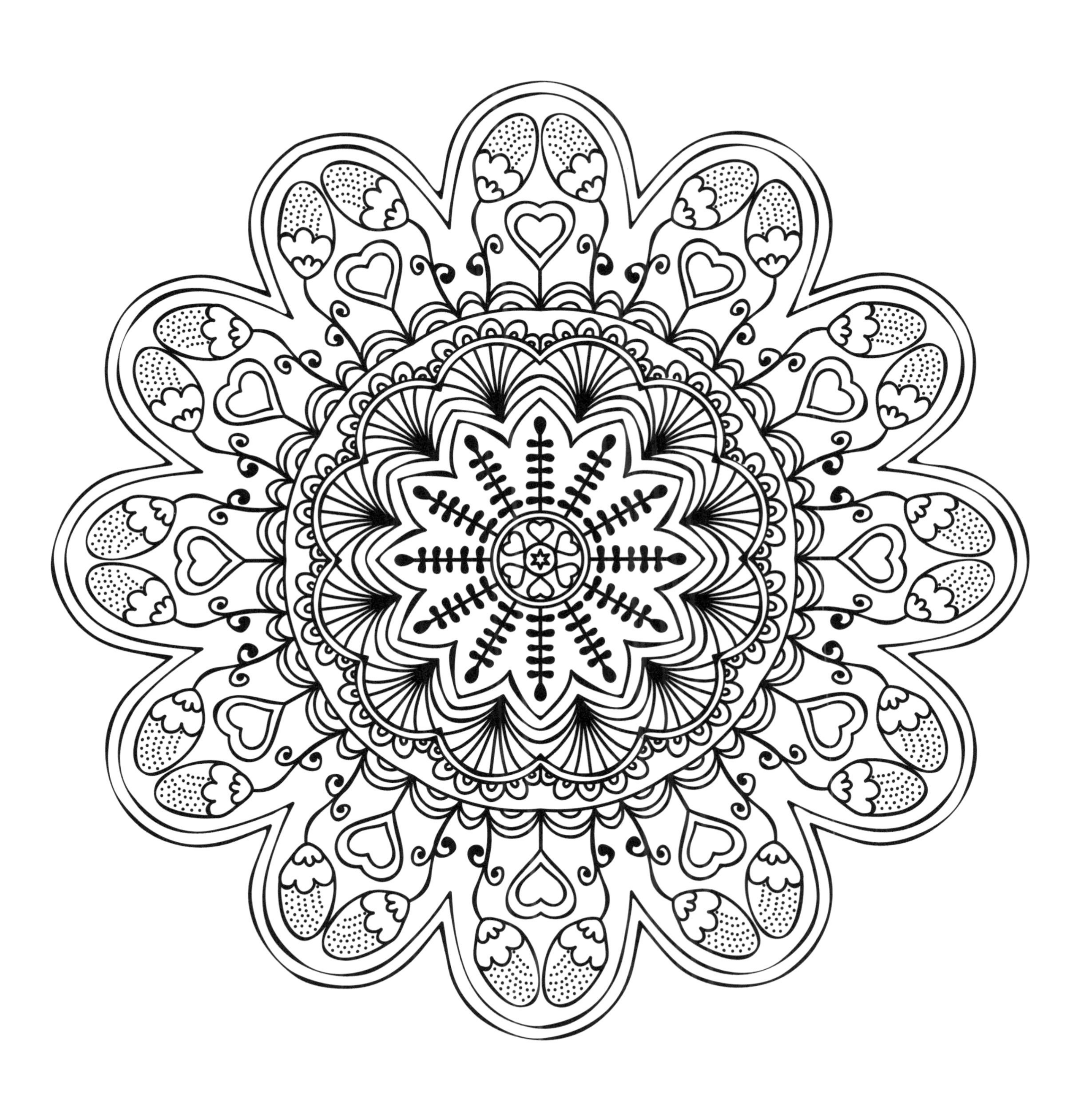

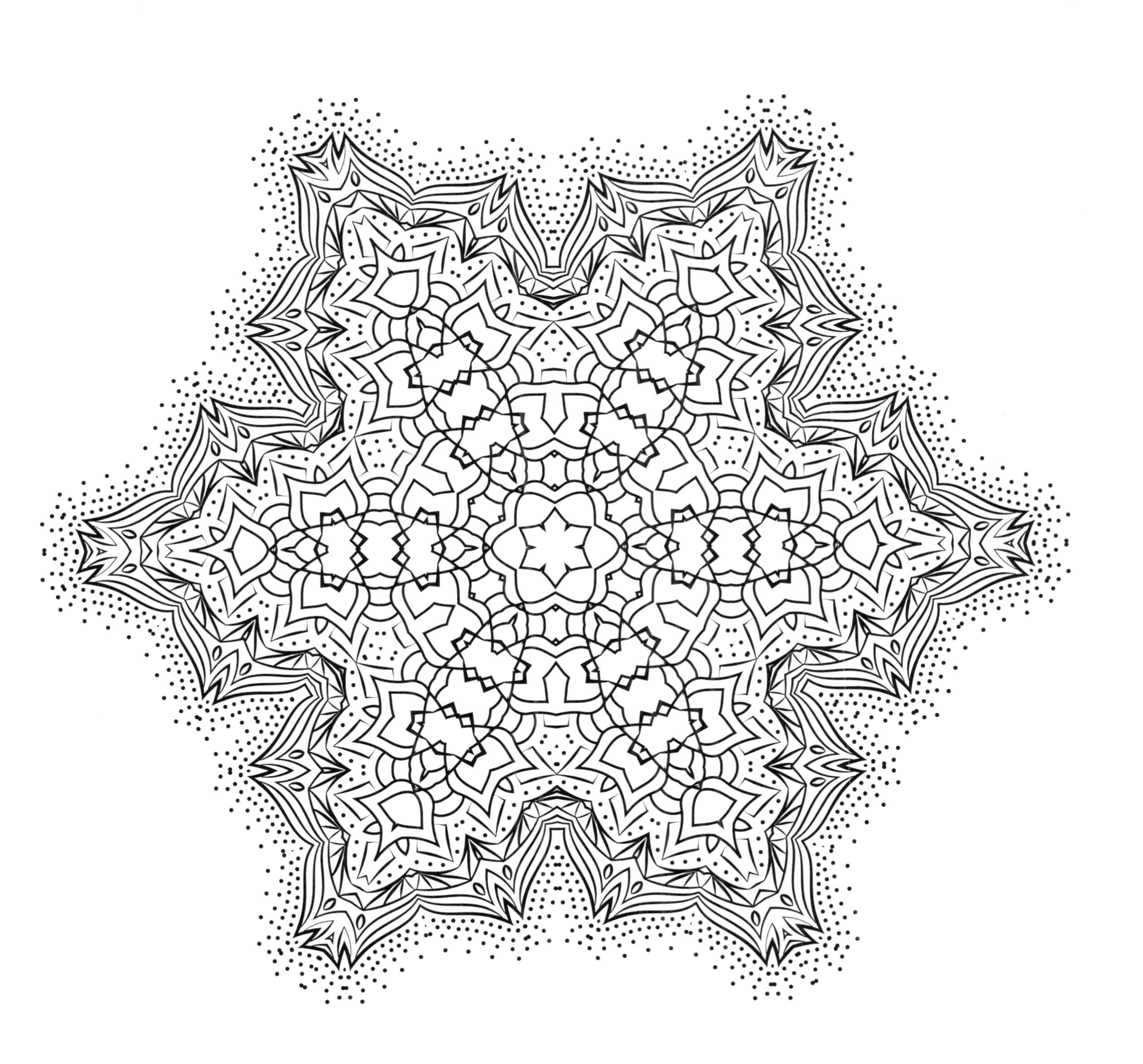

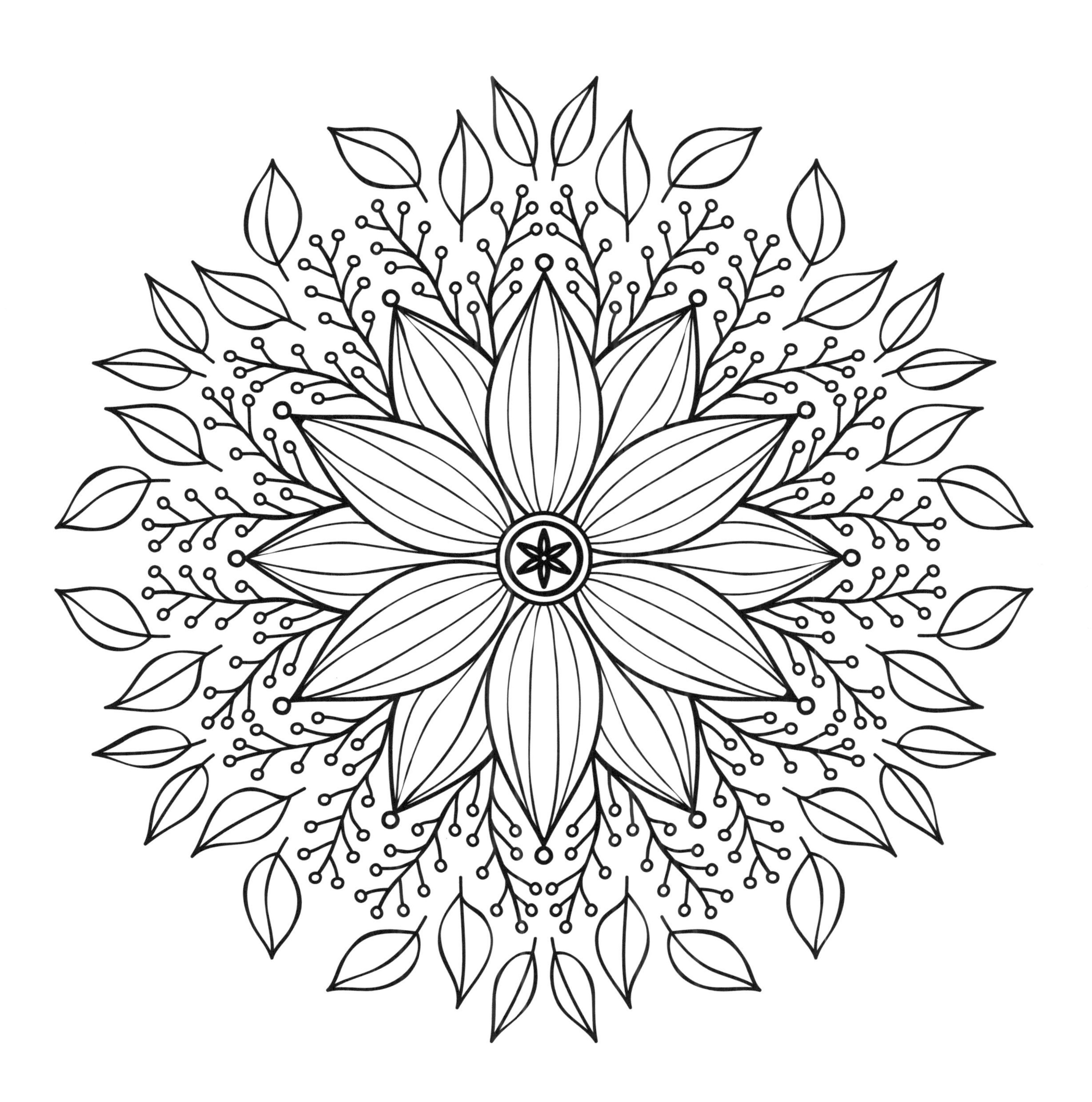

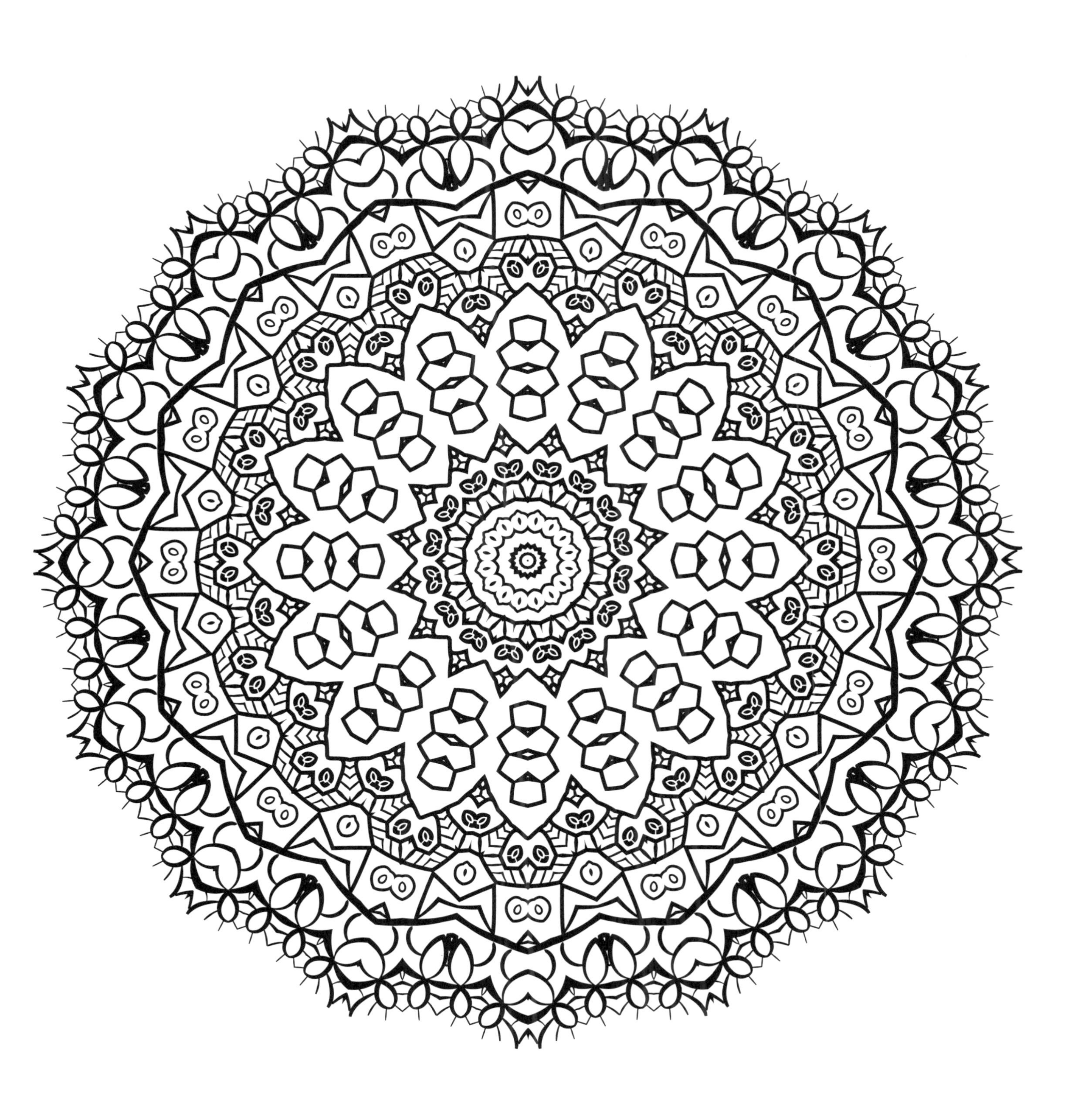

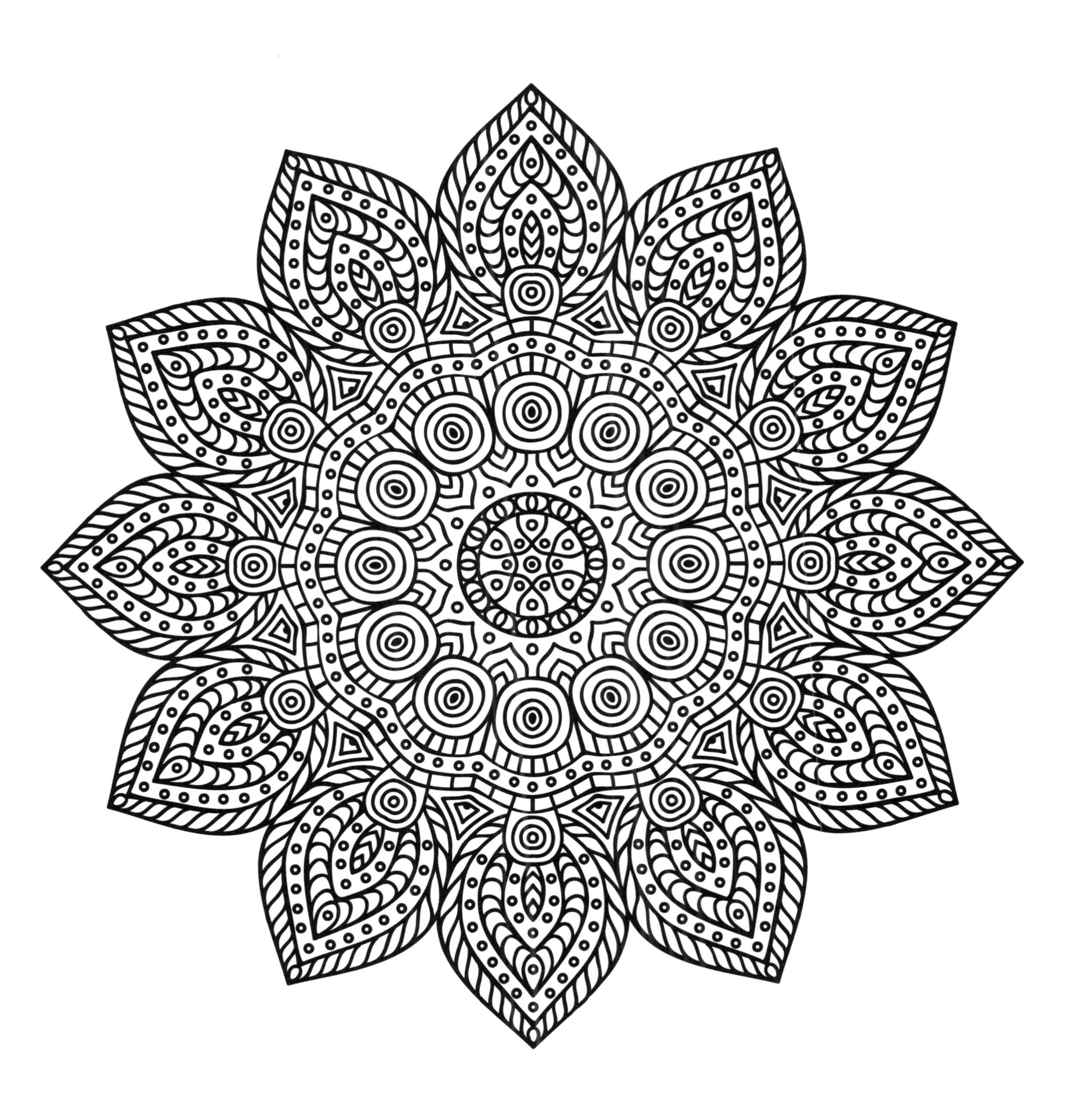

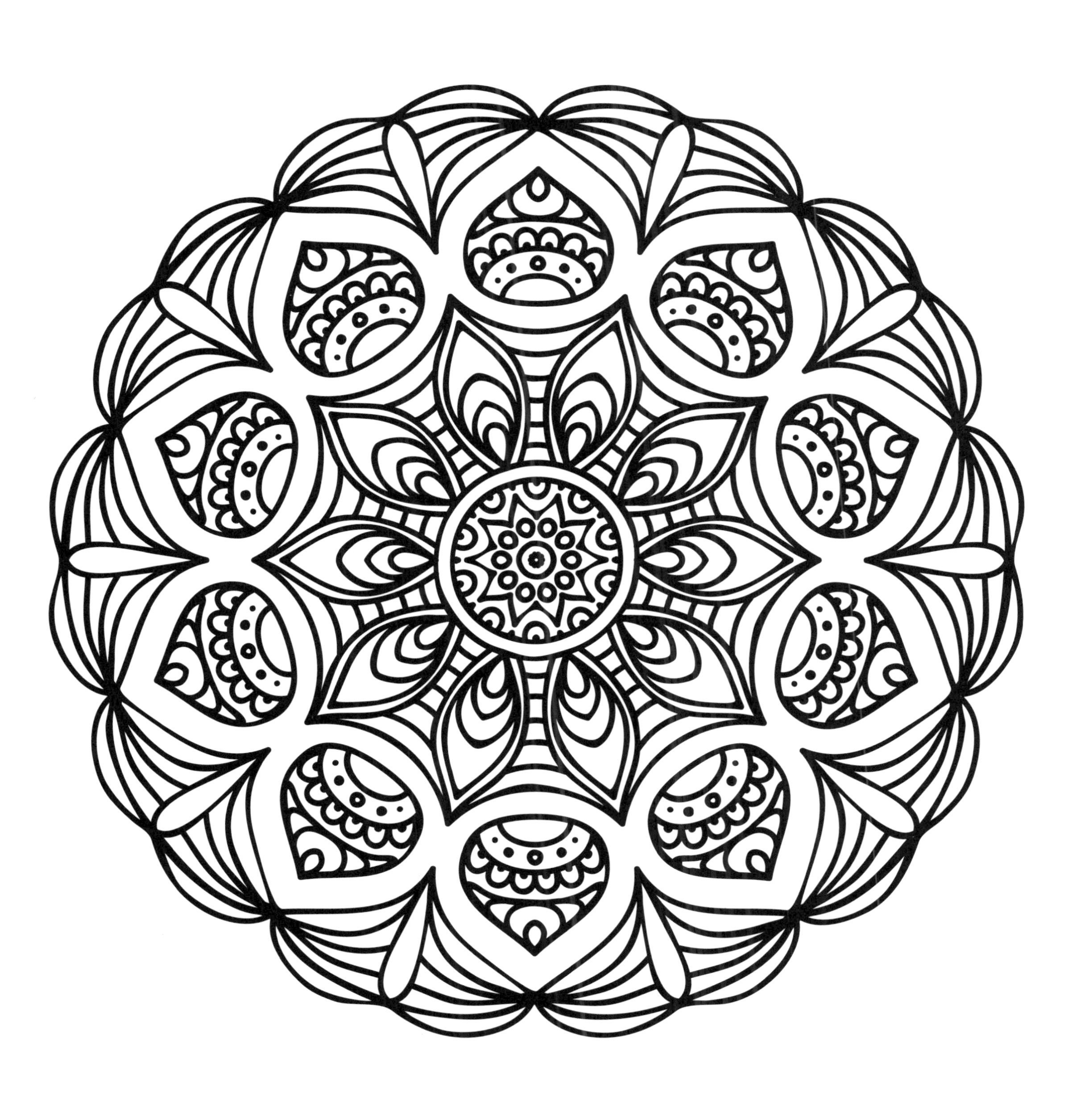

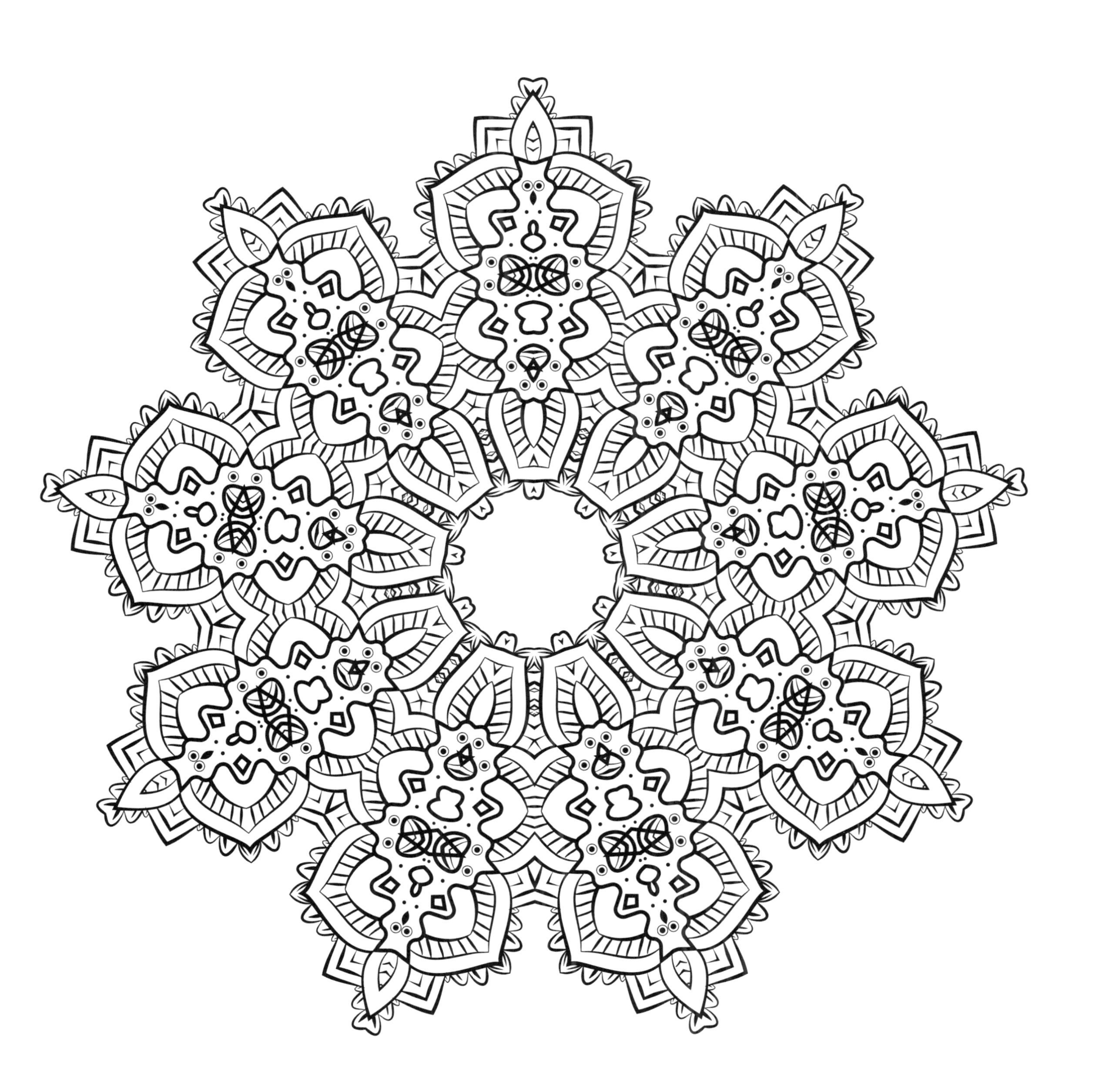

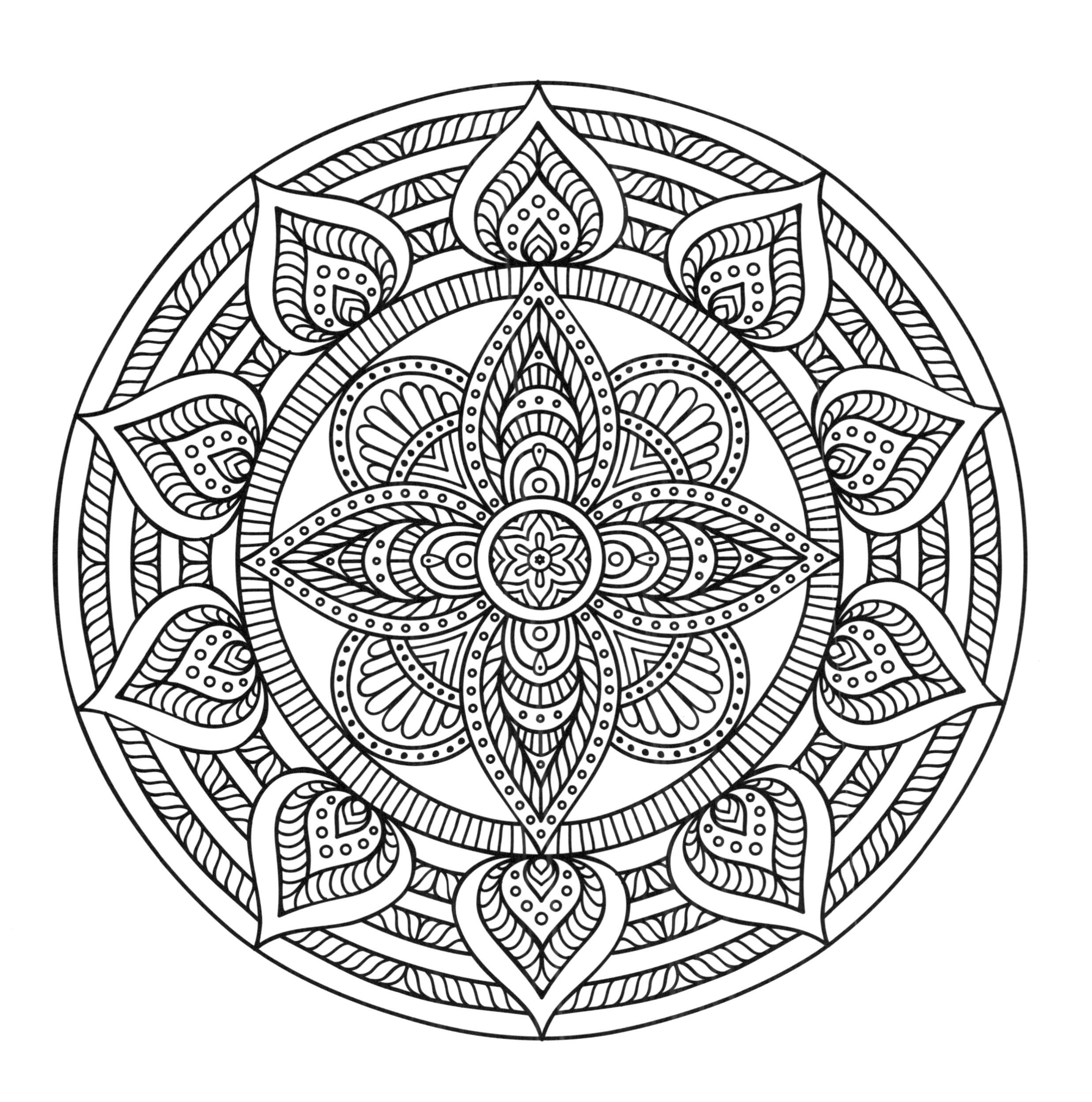

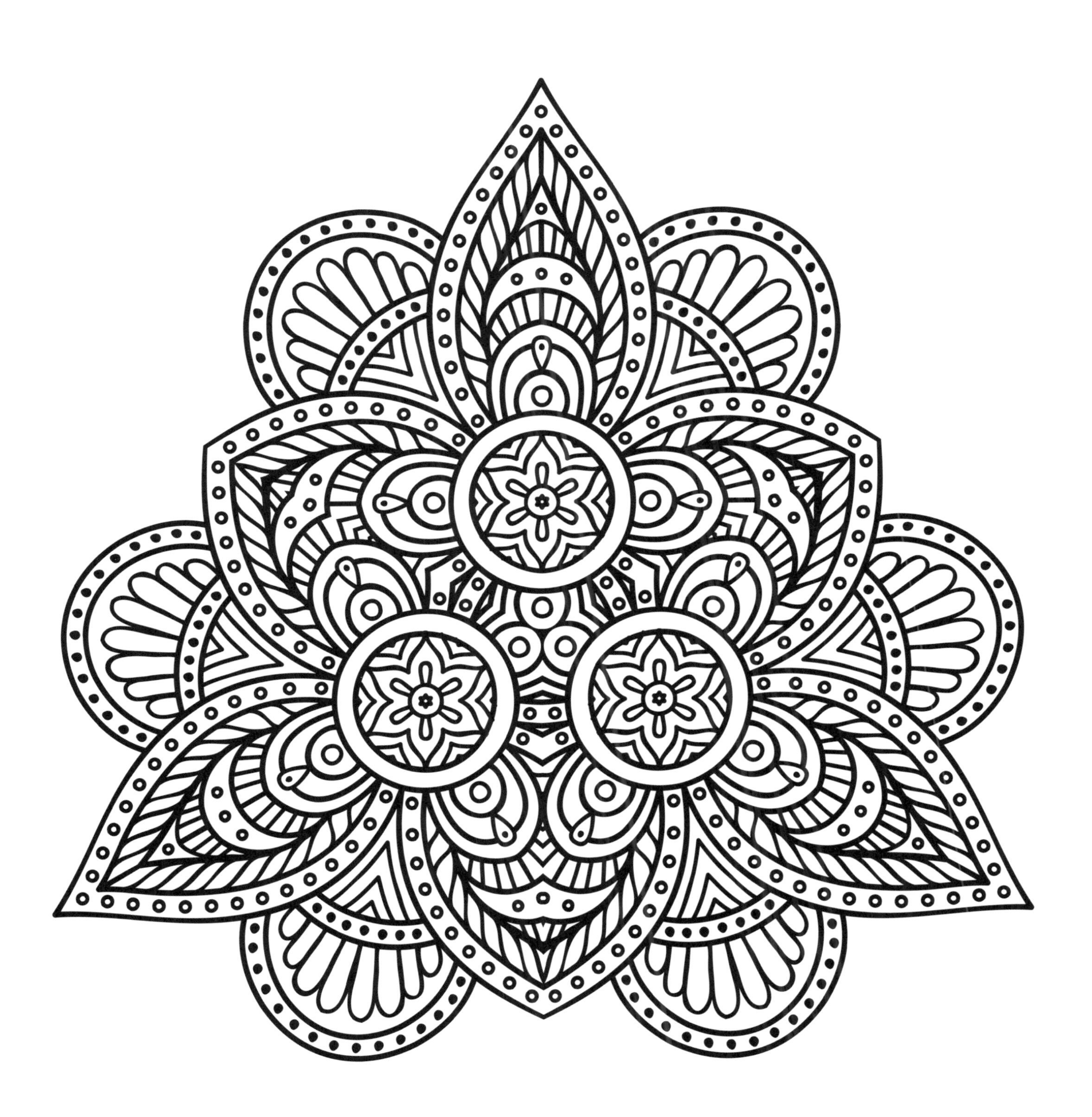

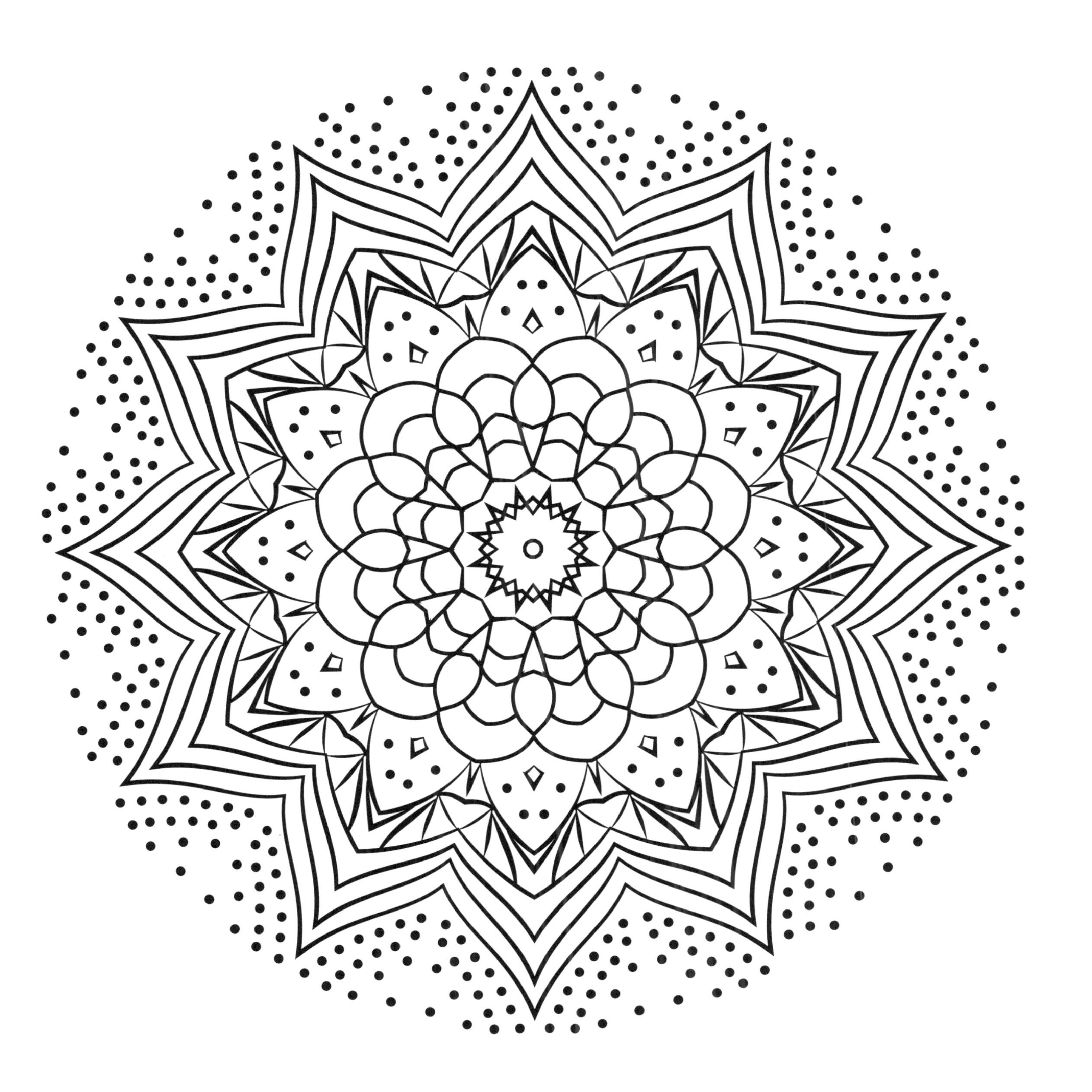

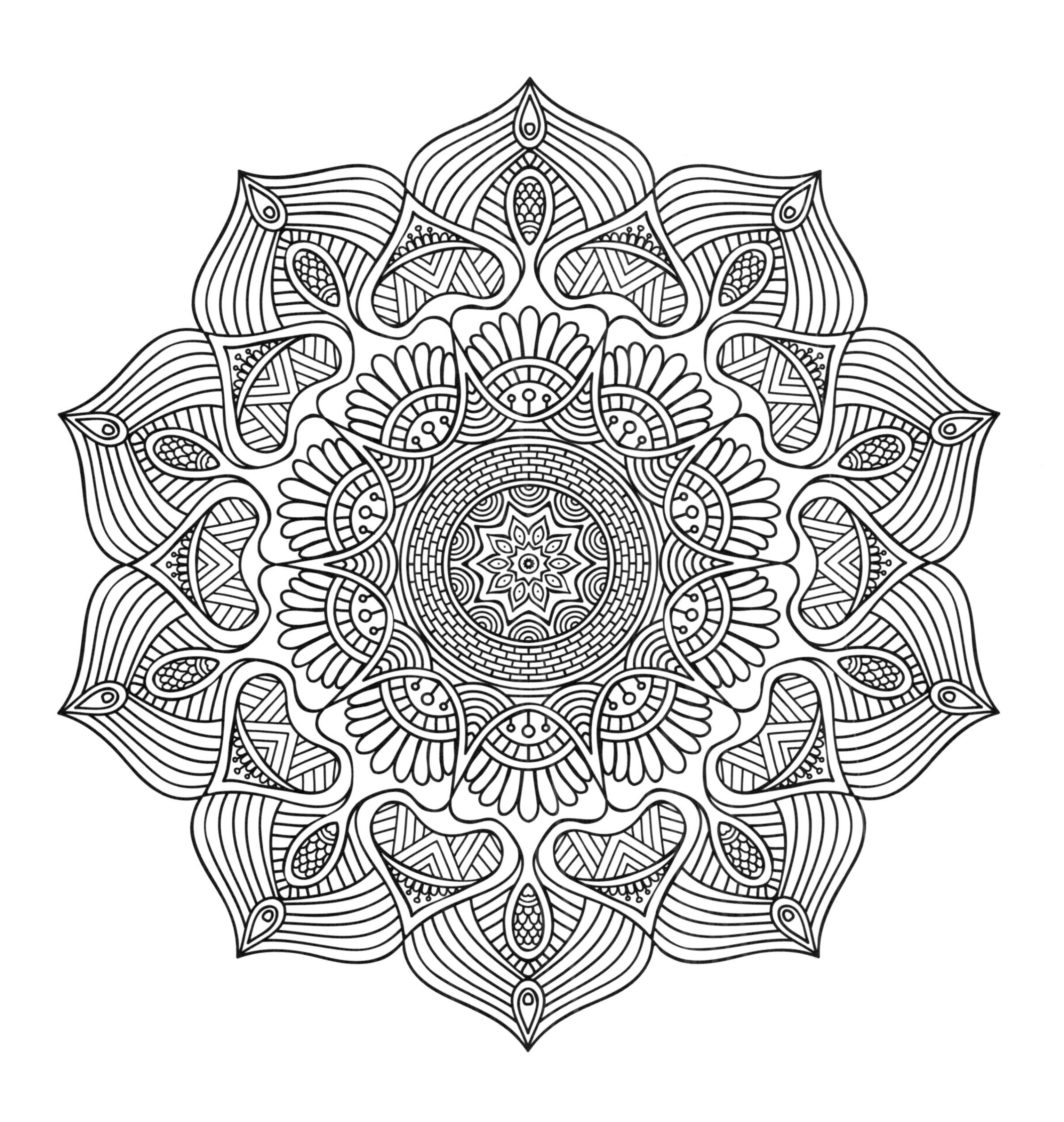

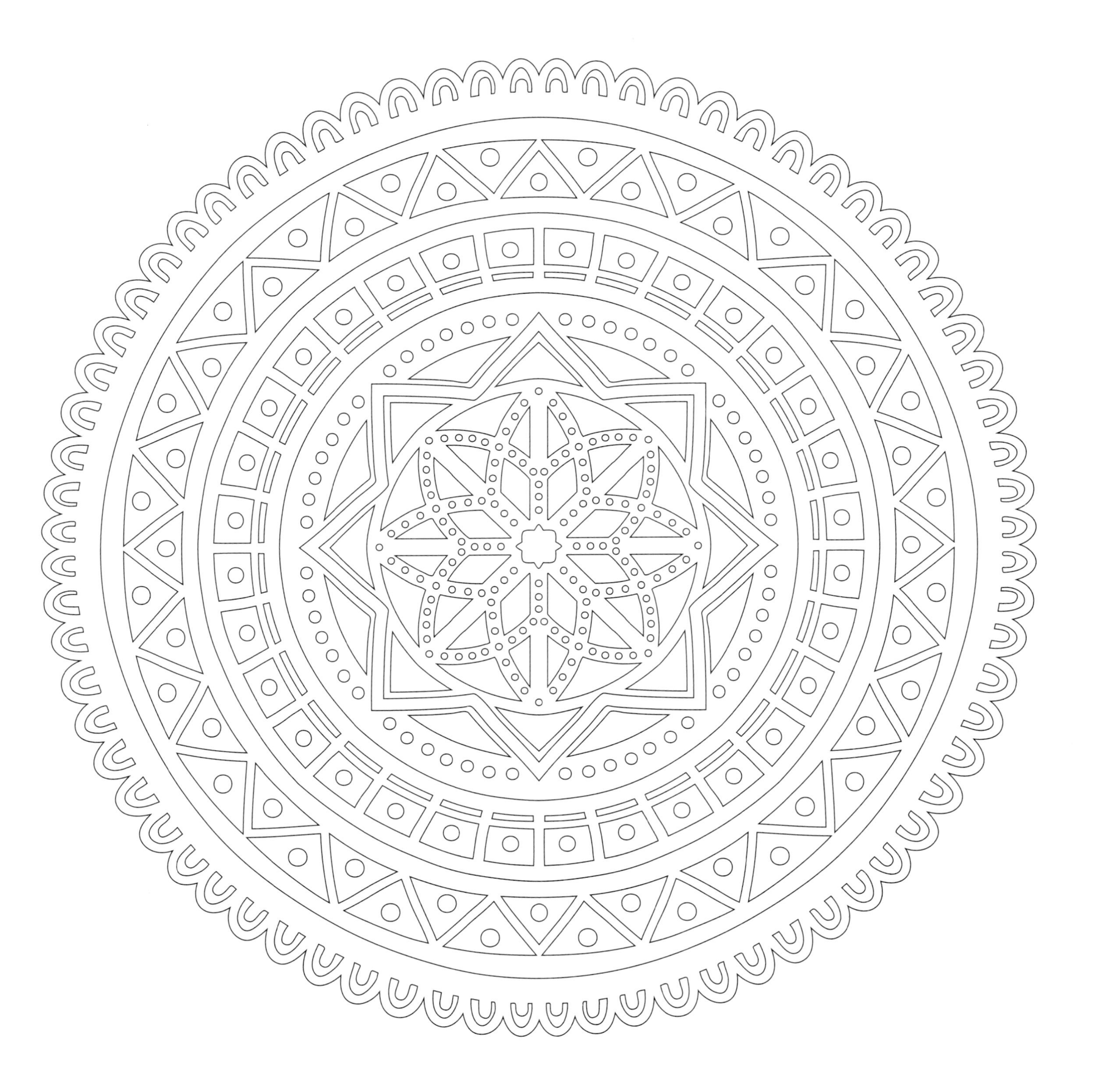

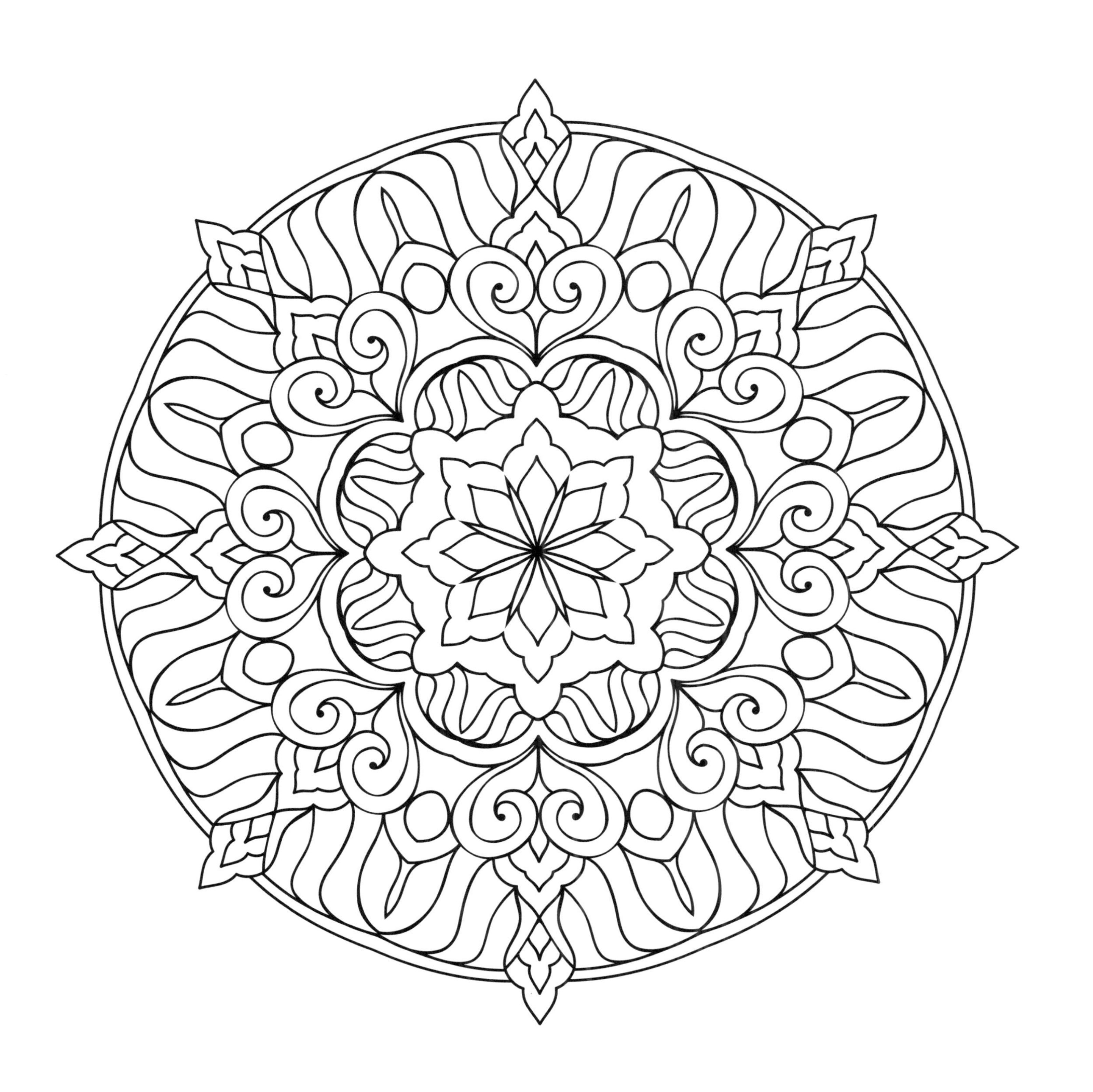

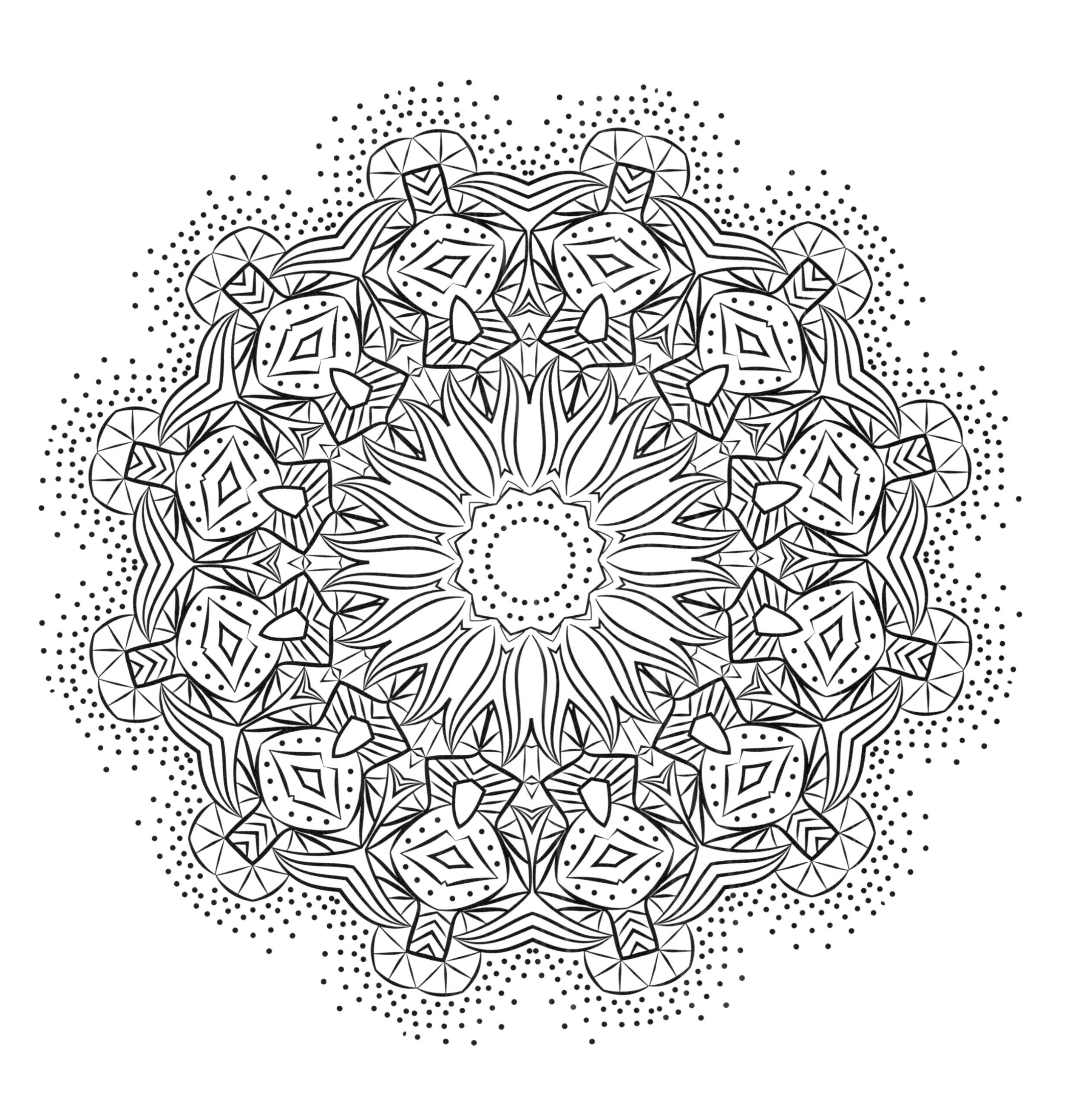

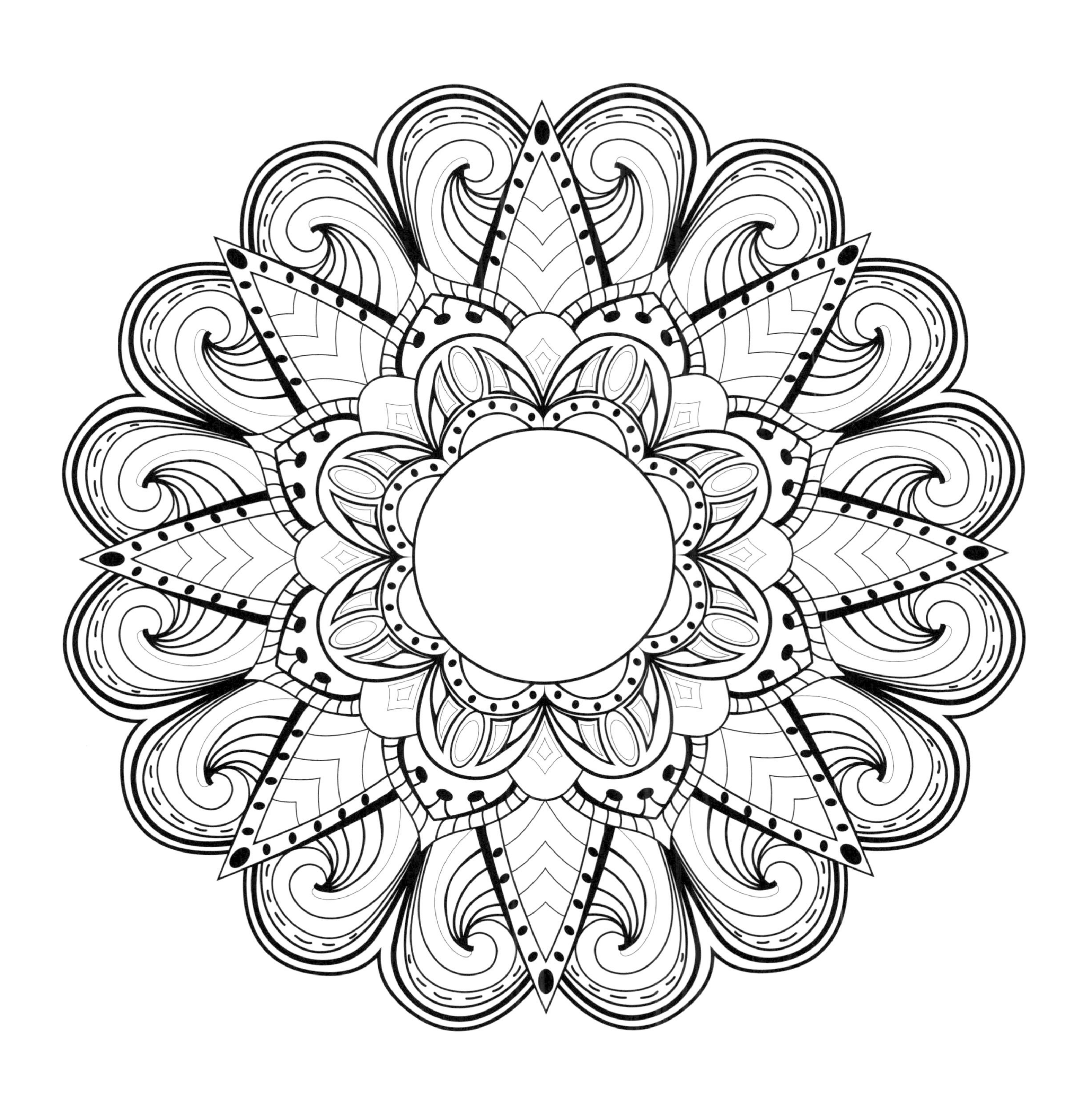